THE RISE OF THE
MAMMALS

THE RISE OF THE MAMMALS

DR MICHAEL BENTON

THE APPLE PRESS

A QUARTO BOOK

Published by The Apple Press
6 Blundell Street
London N7 9BH

Copyright © 1991 Quarto Publishing plc

ISBN 1 85076 347 X

This book was designed and produced by
Quarto Publishing plc
The Old Brewery, 6 Blundell Street
London N7 9BH

Senior Editor: Kate Kirby
Editors: Steve Parker, Maggi McCormick
Art Editor: Philip Gilderdale

Designer: Tony Paine

Illustrators: Graham Rosewarne, Jim Robins, Janos Marffy,
Sally Launder, David Kemp

Picture research: Arlene Bridgewater, Jane Lambert

Art Director: Nick Buzzard

Special thanks to Steve Page

Typeset in Great Britain by ABC Typesetting Ltd,
Bournemouth
Manufactured in Hong Kong by Regent Publishing
Services Limited
Printed in Hong Kong by Leefung-Asco Printers Limited

CONTENTS

INTRODUCTION

Mammals are one of the most diverse and important groups of animals in the world today. They are hairy, backboned animals – creatures such as mice, cats, dogs, horses, elephants, hedgehogs and monkeys. They play major roles in many habitats on land, from camels in deserts to polar bears on ice fields. They are also important in the sea in the shape of seals and whales, and in the air as bats. Indeed, mammals are more significant on Earth today than ever before – since human beings are typical mammals. The fossil record shows, however, that the mammals have not always dominated our planet. The "Age of Mammals" began about 65 million years ago. Although mammals first appeared as early as 220 million years ago, they only took their leading roles in the animal kingdom after the extinction of the dinosaurs. For the first 150 million years of their existence they were insignificant animals, mostly smaller than weasels, hiding by day and creeping about at night in the undergrowth. They would have been hardly visible to a time-traveller who returned to the "Age of Dinosaurs".

First fossil finds

We know about ancient animals such as dinosaurs and early mammals because of fossils. Fossils are bones and other hard parts, like teeth and shells, which become buried in rocks and turn to stone. Fossil bones

Early illustrations often include a mixture of genuine fossils and other fabulous objects. This illustration of Swiss finds, published by Erasmi Francisci in 1668, includes real fossil sponges and corals (top left, bottom left), but also a supposed lizard in a rock (middle right), some "Japanese cross crabs" (middle left), a dolphin with corals on its back (middle right), and indeed a coral growing from a human skull (middle bottom). Most remarkable is the image of the Virgin Mary and Jesus (top right) supposedly found within a stone from the Gotteswalde in Switzerland!

of mammals were doubtless first found long ago by prehistoric humans, especially in the caves and coastal regions where they lived. We shall probably never know what they thought about such finds – perhaps they considered them to be the bones of dragons or mythical gods.

The oldest published records of fossil mammals come from the Mediterranean region, where there are layers of rock rich in the fossil bones of elephants, deer and horses from the Miocene epoch (24–5 million years ago).

We have evidence that the Greeks and Romans collected the fossil bones and other remains of prehistoric mammals, and attempted to explain them in terms of the science of their day. A fossil elephant tooth from the island of Kos, about 100 kilometres (60 miles) south-west of Samos, has been found in the ruins of the Asklepeion, a famous medical school. Empedocles (492–432 BC) wrote about large bones which had been found in Sicily, and Pliny noted fossil ivory. The Emperor Augustus owned a collection of large bones from the island of Capri. In most cases, the bones seem to have been those of elephants, but they were generally thought at the time to be from long-gone races of giant humans. The Roman philosopher Aelianus recorded his views of such bones from the island of Samos, in the Aegean sea:

"Ephorion says in his memoirs that in ancient

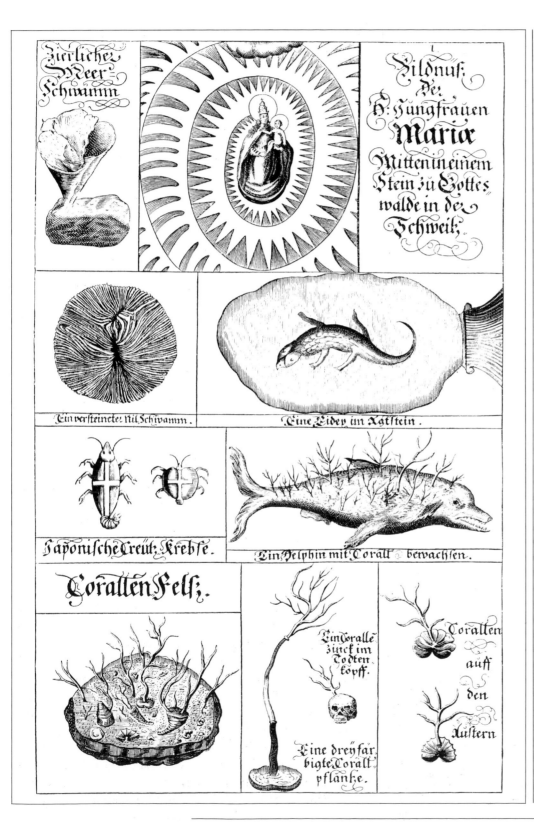

times Samos became uninhabited because of the appearance of great fierce beasts which prevented the people from travelling. These beasts were called Neades, and they could fracture the earth with the sound of their voices alone. The people of Samos had a proverb: to scream louder than the Neades. The author says that even now one can see huge bones of these beasts."

Another philosopher, Plutarch, argued that these huge bones belonged to the Amazons, mythical female warriors who had been slaughtered on Samos by Dionysius.

Giants on earth and Medieval science

The existence of giants remained the favourite explanation of huge fossil mammal bones during the Middle Ages and even the Renaissance. There were several reasons for this.

Firstly, the Bible supports the notion. In Genesis, it says that "there were giants in those days", when talking of the period before the Flood. Secondly, there was a great fascination among philosophers and the public with giants, monsters and dragons. Less was known of the world then, and it would not have seemed ridiculous in Medieval times to regard a three-metre-high (10 feet) human being as any more un-usual than tall stories about giraffes or elephants.

Thirdly, the study of modern mammals, especially their comparative anatomy (the way their bodies are constructed, and similarities between different species), was in a very undeveloped and unsophisti-cated state. There was little detailed knowledge about the variations in the skeletons and other parts of living animals, that would allow scientists to compare them accurately to fossils.

This last point may seem strange to us today. Surely a Medieval philosopher could have opened up and dissected modern animals, in order to compare their bones with those of a fossil animal? The principles of comparative anatomy seem very obvious nowadays. We can see how, and why, closely related animals have similar structures in their bodies.

Even quite distantly related creatures share equiv-alent parts, although the detailed shape or form has changed. For example, the thigh bone of a modern

elephant is essentially the same as that of a fossil elephant. The many bones in the human hand can be compared one by one with those of a fossil human, and even with those of a frog or a dinosaur. However, Medieval scientists did not have the framework of the theory of evolution in which to work. One of the great triumphs of evolutionary theory was to make such relationships obvious and understandable.

From the horse's mouth

Difficult though it is, we can get an impression of the minds of Medieval scientists from a story related by Francis Bacon (1561–1626), the greatest Medieval philosopher of science:

"In the year of our Lord 1432 there arose a grievous quarrel among the brethren [community of friars or monks] over the number of teeth in the mouth of a horse. For thirteen days the disputation raged without ceasing. All of the ancient books and chronicles were fetched out, and wondrous, ponderous erudition such as was never before heard of in this region was made manifest.

At the beginning of the fourteenth day a youthful friar of goodly bearing asked his learned superiors for permission to add a word, and straightway, to the wonderment of the disputants, whose deep wisdom he sore vexed, he beseeched them to unbend in a manner coarse and unheard-of and to look in the open mouth of a horse and find the answer to their questionings. At this, their dignity being grievously hurt, they waxed exceeding wroth: and joining in a mightly uproar, they flew upon him and smote him, hip and thigh, and cast him out forthwith. For said they, surely Satan hath tempted this bold neophyte [trainee friar] to declare unholy and unheard-of ways of finding the truth, contrary to all the teachings of the fathers."

Saints, dragons and unicorns

Knowledge of fossil mammal finds increased dramatically after Medieval times, with the spread of printing. Fossil elephant skulls – which have a large oval-shaped opening near the top for the nostrils, at the root of the fleshy trunk – became the basis for myths of the Cyclops, a one-eyed giant human. In Italy, a mammoth molar tooth was venerated as a relic of Saint Christopher, while in Germany, an elephant vertebra (backbone element) was ascribed to another saint.

Other fossil mammal bones were said to be from dragons. The skull of a woolly rhinoceros was found in 1335 near Klagenfurt, southern Austria. It resided for many years in the town hall, and it formed the basis for a local legend of the Klagenfurt "Lindwurm". Indeed, a sculpture of this mythical dragon was erected in the town in 1636, complete with wings and a rhinoceros-like head! This is said to be the oldest known flesh reconstruction of an extinct animal.

Dragons have been popular in other cultures. The fossil teeth of horses, pigs, deer and other mammals, dating from the last 20 million years, have formed part of the medicinal trade in China for thousands of years. Powdered remains are still used as medicines today. The teeth and bones were found in caves, sink holes and similar places, excavated, and ground to form potions and remedies. They were regarded as the remains of benevolent dragons, and the medicines derived from them were said to be helpful in preventing constipation, nightmares and epilepsy, as well as diseases of the heart, kidneys, intestines and liver. Dragon-bone Hill, near Beijing in China, yielded fossils now known to be from our predecessor *Homo erectus*, famous as "Peking Man".

Fossil mammal bones are also associated with European legends of the unicorn, a horse with a horn on its forehead. The legend may have come originally from sightings of the Indian rhinoceros with its large nose horn, and it was reinforced by the long twisted tusk of the marine narwhal (like other whales, a kind of mammal). Fossil bones and teeth of mammals found in caves in Germany were said to be those of the unicorn, and they too supposedly had medicinal properties. Some early attempts at the reconstruction of fossil skeletons were made to look like unicorns, such as the fanciful beast conjured up by the German scientist Gottfried Wilhelm von Leibniz (1646–1716), based on the bones of a mammoth!

The problem of extinction

The large fossil bones of long-gone mammals continued to be explained as mythological animals by philosophers and scientists up to about 1750. Some scientists stuck to these interpretations even as late as 1850. Even today, reports of living giant apes, yetis, bigfoots, lake creatures and sea monsters show that these kinds of views still exist. There were also arguments about whether such remains were "sports of nature", set in the rocks by the Devil to tempt us into disbelieving the Bible.

However, for most scientists, the eighteenth century saw major advances towards a more modern scientific interpretation of extinct mammals. Gradually, it dawned on the scientific community that fossils which looked like bones actually were bones, of dead animals. But the acceptance that fossils represented dead animals did not mean that

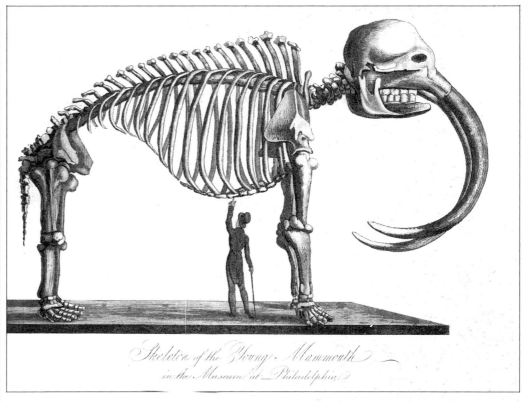

Skeleton of the Young Mammouth in the Museum at Philadelphia

An early illustration of a reconstructed fossil mammal (above), the skeleton of a "young Mammouth" exhibited in Philadelphia, USA, in the early nineteenth century. In fact it is a mastodon, a different kind of elephant altogether from the mammoths, and typical of the last three million years in North America. The reconstruction is fairly accurate, but the tusks have been fitted the wrong way round (they should point up), and the man must be a midget, since the skeleton's true height is 3.5 metres (11 feet).

such creatures were extinct forms; that is, species that have completely died out.

There was a heated debate during the latter part of the eighteenth century about extinction, and fossil mammals figured prominently in its resolution. The traditional view was that extinction would mean God had failed in His creation, and therefore no species of plant or animal could ever die out completely. Fossils tended to be linked to modern species, as far as possible. With a little imagination, most of the mammal bones found in Europe could be compared closely with those of modern horses, deer, bears, elephants and other species. So there was little problem. However, explorations in North America were to challenge this view.

Teeth and thighs

The discovery of a tooth of a North American mastodon, an extinct kind of elephant, was published in France in 1756. This was part of a collection of what we now know to be mastodon remains, made on the Ohio River in 1740 by Baron

Charles de Longueuil. He was a major in the French army, which was then engaged in fighting the British for control of Canada. English settlers also sent bones from this area back to London. The large collections of mastodon teeth and bones provided the scientists of France and England with a test-case with which to debate the idea of extinction, in the 1760s.

The French scientist Louis-Jean-Marie Daubenton (1716–1800) showed that the thigh bone of the American animal was essentially the same as that of a modern elephant and also of a Siberian mammoth. However, he said that the mastodon teeth were those of a hippopotamus, since they were so different from those of modern elephants.

The British anatomist William Hunter (1718–1783) argued that all the bones and teeth belonged to a single animal, termed the "American *incognitum*" meaning the unknown American. It had the bones of an elephant, but the teeth of a carnivore. He noted, significantly: "If this animal was indeed carnivorous, which I believe cannot be doubted, though we may as philosophers regret it, as men we cannot but thank Heaven that its whole generation is probably extinct."

Although Hunter was wrong in insisting that the mastodon was a carnivore, he was correct in saying it was extinct. However, many scientists of the day were still unwilling to accept the idea of extinction. Surely the American *incognitum* would be found some day, living in one of the unexplored parts of America, Africa or Asia. The same hopeful argument was made for the mammoth, then known from abundant remains in Siberia, and for other large mammals coming to light in different parts of the world. These included the giant ground sloth from South America, and a variety of horse and tapir-like creatures from older rocks of the Paris basin in France.

The turning point: Hutton and Cuvier

Two major advances in scientific thinking were made about 1800, which allowed scientists to understand fossil mammals in a modern way. It was realized that the Earth was extremely ancient; and

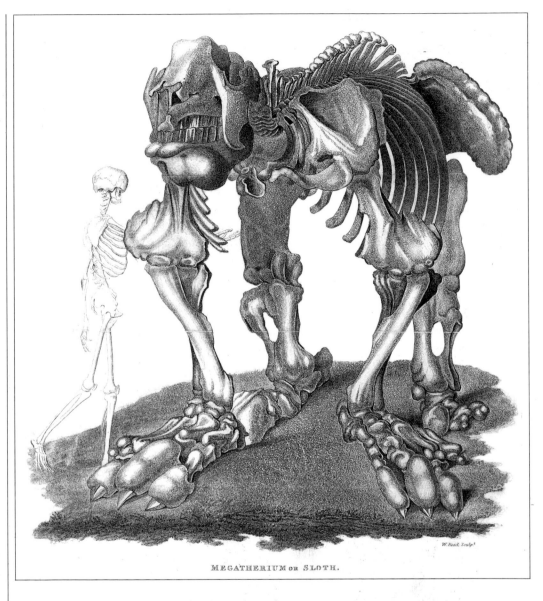

MEGATHERIUM or SLOTH.

The first reasonably accurate reconstruction of a fossil mammal was produced in 1796, based on giant bones sent to Spain from South America. These were recognized by Cuvier, the brilliant French anatomist, as the bones of an extinct giant ground sloth, which he named Megatherium americanum. *This huge animal browsed on trees, and it could rear up on its hindquarters.*

the techniques of comparative anatomy became firmly established.

A literal reading of the Bible implies that the Earth was created in its modern form in a relatively short time. Before 1750, the church was very powerful, and scientists were required to accept this idea. They had to compress their observations of fossils and rocks into a very short span of prehistoric time. During the French enlightenment, in the second half of the eighteenth century, this was questioned by several philosophers. Ideas of evolution were proposed, but their proponents faced religious problems.

The Scottish agriculturalist and geologist James Hutton (1726–97) collected his geological observations in a book, *Theory of the Earth*, published in 1795. He demonstrated convincingly that the Earth had to be ancient, in order to explain the massively long-term processes of erosion and rock deposition that must have taken place in order to create the rock layers we see today. A long time-scale (we now know the Earth formed some 4,500 million years ago) allowed enough time for all fossils to be fitted in, and for extinction to have occurred.

The French naturalist Baron Georges Cuvier (1769–1832) is credited with establishing comparative anatomy as the basis for zoology, the study of living animals, and paleontology, the study of fossils. By 1800, he had studied many of the fossil mammals and reptiles known at the time, and he presented accurate reconstructions of the skeletons, and logical

Georges, Baron Cuvier (1769–1832), pictured in his later years, when he had become a distinguished and high-ranking official in French political life. He pioneered the techniques of comparative anatomy, which show how related animals share basic design similarities, and that their bodies are modified to suit their functions and lifestyle. Cuvier is most noted for his work with fossils, and the famous demonstrations of his ability to predict the nature of an entire skeleton from a single bone.

explanations of their former owners' relationships and habits. His skills were based on a thorough study of the bones and flesh of modern animals, and a realization that evolution used similar "design solutions" when fashioning animals and their adaptations.

It is said that Cuvier could take any bone, recent or ancient, and reconstruct the whole animal from which it came. This might smack of showmanship, but it is founded firmly in the two chief principles by which paleontologists and biologists have worked ever since. The more closely related animals are to one another, the more similar they are in all respects; and, similar structures in different animals usually perform the same functions.

The age of discovery

Although many fossils of mammals had been collected before 1800, most of them were misinterpreted, and the remains were often mistreated or lost. After 1800, a number of major scientific beliefs – such as the possibility of extinction, the great age of the Earth, and the rise of comparative anatomy – permitted scientists to study fossil mammals in a constructive way. They started to leave their armchairs and go out to search for specimens. Later scientific and social developments in the early part of the nineteenth century hastened the rate of discovery. For example, a growing public interest in geology and ancient life led to the foundation of local museums throughout Europe, and the formation of networks of keen amateur collectors. The growing acceptance of the theory of evolution, after the publication of Charles Darwin's *On the Origin of Species* in 1859, gave a major impetus to the study of fossils with a view to drawing evolutionary trees showing the relationships of groups of animals, both living and extinct.

Dozens of species of mammals from the past 65 million years (the Cenozoic era) were excavated from the rich deposits of Europe. In 1827, the first mammal from the Mesozoic era (245–65 million years ago, the "Age of Dinosaurs") was found in England. The mammalian lineage was extended even further back in time by fascinating collections of fossils made in South Africa in the 1840s.

Andrew Geddes Bain (1797–1864), a Scottish engineer employed to build roads, found numerous skulls and skeletons in the Karoo Basin of South Africa. These were eventually sent to London, where Sir Richard Owen (1804-92), the leading British anatomist of Victorian times, described them in 1854. He noted similarities of these unusual fossils with various groups of reptiles, but spotted that their teeth were like those of mammals. These were the first discovered mammal-like reptiles, a major group that existed during the Late Carboniferous, Permian and Triassic periods (320–208 million years ago). They included the ancestors of the true mammals.

Further very important discoveries of fossil mammals in the first half of the nineteenth century included fossil apes from France, a fossil whale from Alabama, USA (found in 1834), and ground sloths, giant anteaters and other strange mammals from South America, collected by Charles Darwin (1809–82) himself in 1833.

Some of the greatest additions to our knowledge of fossil mammals came from North America, especially during the heroic age of fossil collecting in the last quarter of the nineteenth century. The great paleontologists Edward Cope and Othniel Marsh vied with each other to produce ever more spectacular animals from the Badlands of the Midwest. Tinoceras ingens was a giant, extinct, horned plant-eater dating back some 40 million years, first described by Marsh.

Money and rivalry

After 1850, the rate of discovery increased apace as professional explorers continued to visit ever more remote parts of the world, and as each country began to build up major national museums for their collections of fossil specimens. Money became available to pay professors and curators, and funds were spent on displaying the remarkable skeletons to the public. Personal rivalries among collectors also stimulated herculean efforts in the discovery and description of fossil mammals.

Edward Drinker Cope (1840–97) and Othniel Charles Marsh (1831–99) are probably best known for their collecting of North American dinosaurs, but they both made major contributions to our

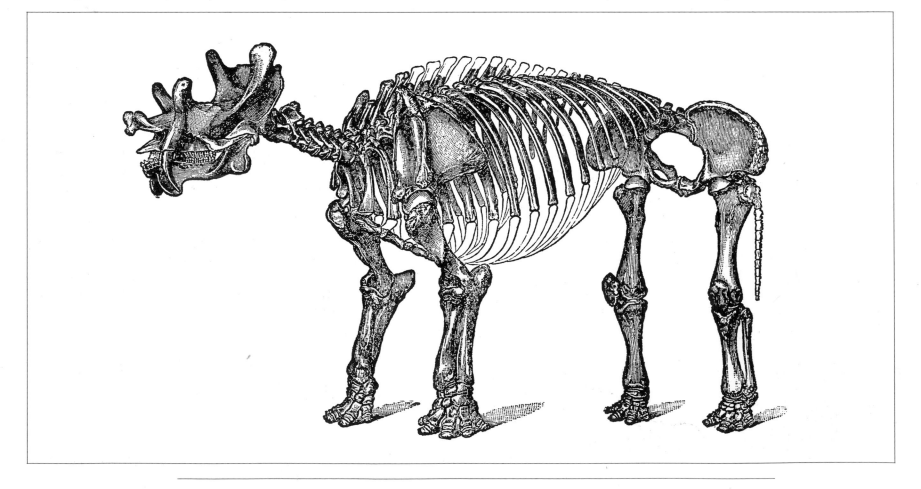

knowledge of fossil mammals. Both men had sufficient funds to pay teams of professional collectors, who operated in the rich "bone beds" of the mid-western USA. Trainloads of the remains of mammals and large dinosaurs were sent to Pennsylvania and Connecticut, where Cope and Marsh respectively tore open the cases and rapidly published descriptions of the remarkable new animals. Since 1900, the tradition of large-scale collecting of fossil mammals has continued in the USA, with teams operating worldwide and discovering hundreds of skeletons.

American and European paleontologists, as well as locally-based scientists, have now built up an extraordinarily detailed knowledge of fossil mammals of the past 65 million years – the Tertiary (65–2) and Quaternary (2–0) periods. Indeed, prehistoric mammals are so well known in many areas that they are used for precision dating of the rocks. However, some parts of the mammalian fossil record – such as Mesozoic mammals and fossil humans – are poorly known, despite vast research efforts. This is probably because the creatures were extremely rare at the time.

One of the first artistic attempts to show what a fossil mammal looked like in real life (above). This is the brontothere Brontops robustus, *from an illustration of the 1890s, based on complete skeletons from the American West. It is depicted as rather rhinoceros-like, and indeed it appears to be distantly related to modern rhinos.*

Edward Drinker Cope (1840–1897), one of the most distinguished paleontologists of the nineteenth century (left). In many ways he was politically less successful than his rival Othniel Marsh, but he was probably a more brilliant scientist. On his desk, behind the pen, is a fossil elephant skull, seen from the front; to its left is a human skull; and to the left of that is the front end of a very strange stuffed animal, possibly an "early horse", made from bits of fur!

Fossil mammals today

Current work is greatly extending our knowledge of fossil mammals. Major collecting efforts in Australia and China are filling some of the main geographical gaps with many exciting new finds. New techniques of study, and fresh areas of research interest, are also adding colour to the picture: diets and feeding, movement and locomotion, population dynamics, patterns of evolution, mass extinctions and the like. This present book is intended to give a flavour of what we know about fossil mammals, including our own ancestors, and to explain how we know. The chapters are arranged chronologically, to form the "story of mammal evolution", with emphasis on current paleobiological research and new techniques of study.

Michael Benton

Michael Benton
Bristol, September 1990

THE EVOLUTION OF MAMMALS AND THEIR RELATIVES

This "evolutionary tree" provides a simple summary of the fossil record of the main mammal groups and of their ancestors, the mammal-like reptiles. It is set in the context of the evolution of other major vertebrate groups — birds, reptiles, amphibians and fishes.

This diagram is set against a scale of geological time (marked along the bottom). It is based on the latest scientific information, and it takes the form of a cladogram, which is rather different from the types of evolutionary trees presented in other popular books. The essence of a cladogram is detailed analysis of the features or characters of all the organisms involved. Derived, or advanced, characters are sought that have been inherited from a common ancestor; these link pairs of groups, and hence provide a measure of the closeness of relationship. The cladogram is therefore a tree of relationships.

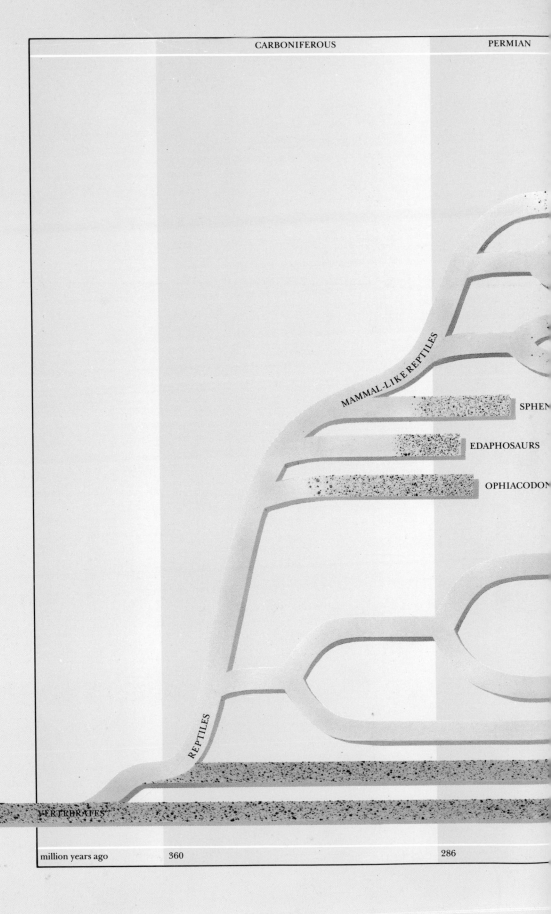

MAMMAL-LIKE REPTILES

SPHEN

EDAPHOSAURS

OPHIACODON

REPTILES

VERTEBRATES

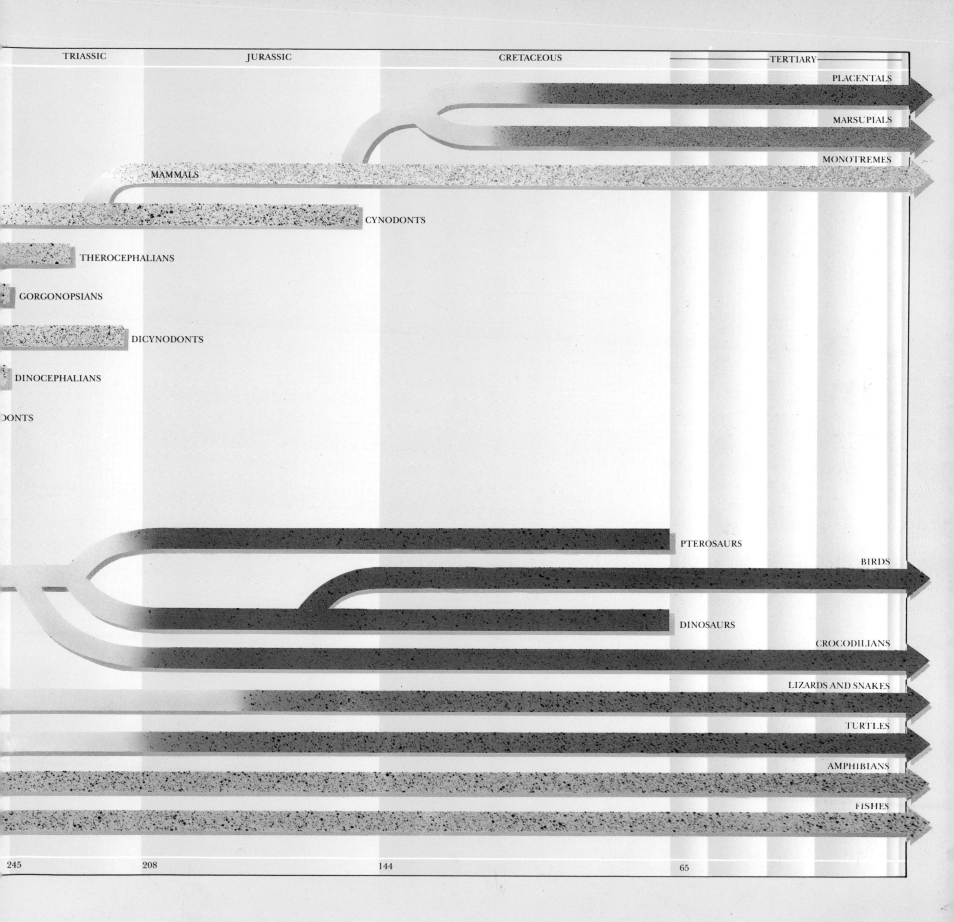

TRIASSIC | JURASSIC | CRETACEOUS | TERTIARY

PLACENTALS

MARSUPIALS

MONOTREMES

MAMMALS

CYNODONTS

THEROCEPHALIANS

GORGONOPSIANS

DICYNODONTS

DINOCEPHALIANS

DONTS

PTEROSAURS

BIRDS

DINOSAURS

CROCODILIANS

LIZARDS AND SNAKES

TURTLES

AMPHIBIANS

FISHES

245 | 208 | 144 | 65

CHAPTER ONE

FROM REPTILE TO MAMMAL

The oldest known specimens of mammals date from the Late Triassic period (about 220 million years ago) of Europe. These were small insectivorous animals, no larger than a mouse. For the next 150 million years, during the "Age of the Dinosaurs", the mammals occupied a variety of niches or life-styles, but did not become larger than cat-sized. It is possible to trace the direct line of evolution, through the diverse and important mammal-like reptiles, in some detail. This provides an understanding of how the mammals evolved, and how they differ from other animals.

The search for common ancestors

Archaeothyris – the oldest known mammal-like reptile – was a lizard-like animal in appearance, and probably in habits, although not in relationships. The skull is 9 centimetres (3½ inches) long, and the whole body was probably about 50 centimetres (1½ feet). *Archaeothyris* had short limbs, but could probably move relatively fast on land. The key feature is a single lower temporal fenestra, a small opening in the bone at the back of the skull. This is the diagnostic character of the Synapsida, the animal grouping which encompasses mammal-like reptiles and mammals. Even though the remains are incomplete, this is proof that *Archaeothyris* is the oldest-known member of our own lineage.

How can such a seemingly minor feature as an opening in the back of a skull give rise to such extravagant claims about evolution? We need to understand how organisms fit into the pattern of evolution, as portrayed by the great

Two entwined skeletons of the mammal-like reptile Diictodon *from the Teekloof Formation, Beaufort Group (Late Permian), from the Karoo Basin, South Africa. One animal lies across the top, with its skull on the right, while the other is curled back on itself towards the bottom left, its skull in the middle. It would be tempting to suggest that a male and female were preserved while mating, but other explanations are much more likely! Probably these two carcasses were washed together into an ancient river and deposited on a sandbank.*

branching tree showing the history of life. We can then see how *Archaeothyris* relates to other mid-Carboniferous amphibians and reptiles.

The study of evolutionary trees, or phylogenies, is carried out today by two main techniques: molecular phylogeny reconstruction, and cladistics. Cladistics is a powerful analytical technique for generating branching tree-like diagrams, called cladograms, that can be translated into phylogenies fairly readily. Cladistics depends on the search for shared derived characters or homologies, which are features that are similar in two or more species and which they inherited from a single ancestor.

The human hand is homologous with that of a cat, a horse, a crocodile, a dinosaur, and even an ancient reptile such as *Archaeothyris*. Our hand is also homologous with the front flipper of a dolphin, and the outer parts of the wing of a bat. Even though these various structures may look very different, the bones are all equivalent. They arose in some distant common ancestor and have been inherited by each group, although evolution has had a hand in reshaping them along the way.

Homologies are contrasted with analogies, which are structures that look very similar in two or more species but which on close inspection can be shown to have very different origins. For example, the wing of a bat is quite different in detail from the wing of a fly, even though the two wing types perform a similar function.

The "higher" land vertebrates – the reptiles, birds, and mammals – arose in the Early Carboniferous period, and branched into three by the beginning of the Late Carboniferous: the Synapsida, Diapsida, and Anapsida.

These three key lines of evolution represent the bulk of land vertebrate evolution over the past 320 million years, and are distinguished by relatively simple features of the skull. The Anapsida have no openings behind the eye socket in the cheek region. The Diapsida have two openings, the temporal openings. The Synapsida have only a lower temporal opening. The different temporal openings appear to be associated with the attachments of jaw muscles, and weight-saving in the skull bones.

The sail-backs

Archaeothyris and other early mammal-like reptiles that came after it, during Late Carboniferous and Early Permian times (320–258 million years ago), are commonly termed the pelycosaurs or "sail-backs". This group includes six fairly well-defined families of both carnivorous and herbivorous reptiles. In some parts of the world, they were the dominant animals of their time.

Although reptiles had arisen in the Early Carboniferous, and the main groups of reptiles were distinct by the beginning of the Late Carboniferous, they did not take over straight away. The amphibians continued to dominate worldwide, with a variety of small, medium and large forms, some adapted to life in fresh waters, and others to a more terrestrial existence. Towards the end of the Carboniferous, however, there were major environmental changes. The vast, lush coal forests of Europe and North America receded and gave way to more arid, desert-like conditions. It seems that many of the primitive amphibians were unable to cope with the shortage of water, and they disappeared. Other amphibian groups lived on through the Permian period, and indeed well into the Age of the Dinosaurs. They later gave rise to the modern amphibian groups – frogs, salamanders and newts – but in the meantime, the reptiles came into dominance on land.

Pelycosaur diversity in Late Carboniferous and Early Permian times gave a foretaste of the later importance of the Synapsida. There were moderate to large-sized reptiles of the ophiacodont type, like *Archaeothyris*, all of which were fish-eaters. *Ophiacodon* itself reached a length of 3 metres (10 feet) and an estimated body weight of 200 kilograms (440 pounds). There were also two or three families of smaller flesh-eating pelycosaurs.

Two pelycosaur families show a remarkable advance in their adaptations. The caseids and edaphosaurids were both herbivorous groups, and they were the first known plant-eating reptiles (and therefore amniotes).

The front half of the fossil skeleton of Aerosaurus wellesi, *from the Early Permian rocks of Texas, USA. This small pelycosaur was a carnivore (note the sharp, slightly curved teeth), and had the proportions of a large lizard.*

Some of the caseids, such as *Cotylorhynchus* from Texas, reached great size, 3–4 metres (10–13 feet) in length. The skull had a peculiar pointed snout, and the teeth were peg-like rather than blade-like, a clear indication of the plant diet. Further, the rib cage was vast, large enough to accommodate the massive gut of a herbivore. The head was preposterously small when compared to the rest of the body, and looks as if it belonged to an animal one-quarter the size! Carnivores, on the other hand, always have relatively large heads in order to cope with struggling prey.

The edaphosaurids, such as *Edaphosaurus*, showed similar adaptations to plant-eating, but they had an unusual feature which gives the popular name to the pelycosaur group. There was a massive sail down the middle of the back. This sail was supported by elongated bony spines on the vertebrae (backbones) of the back. The spines formed a regular rise-and-fall series from the back of the neck to the tail. They were clearly covered with skin in life because there are traces of blood vessel canals preserved on the surface of the fossilized bones.

Reptile radiators

The largest pelycosaur group, the carnivorous sphenacodontids such as *Dimetrodon*, also had sails. But these were rather different in construction and probably evolved independently from the sails of the edaphosaurids – that is, they were (in the language of cladistics) analogies and not homologies. There has been much speculation on the

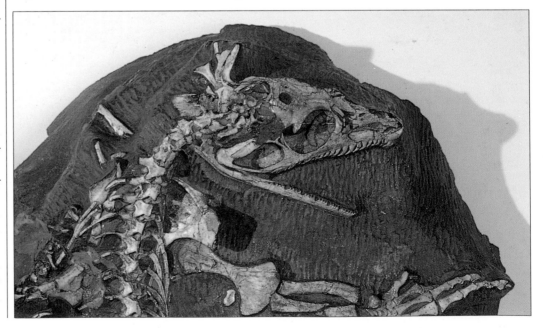

purpose of the sail. The rich supply of blood to the sail, as indicated by the many blood-vessel canals set into the fossil bone, gives a clue to its function. Most paleontologists accept that the sail acted as a heat-exchange mechanism.

The pelycosaurs, being typical reptiles, were ectotherms. This means they controlled their body temperature by external means, such as basking in the sun or cooling off in dark caves. (Birds and mammals are endotherms, and maintain a constant body temperature by generating heat within the body.) The sail would have acted to speed up the transfer of heat, like a giant living radiator. In the morning, a cool *Dimetrodon* would creep out into the Sun and absorb heat from the rays, through the sail into its body. In the heat of the day, the sail would give out extra warmth and stop the mammal-like reptile from overheating. In other words, the sail might have given *Dimetrodon* an edge in the hunting stakes. It would have warmed up to activity temperature faster than its sail-less brethren, and thus have been able to catch prey species which were still too cool to move about rapidly. The herbivorous *Edaphosaurus* could have escaped, since it also had a sail. One unsolved problem with all of this is that most pelycosaurs did not have a sail – only the two rather common genera just described!

(Continued on page 22.)

The front foot of the giant, sail-backed, mammal-like reptile Cotylorhynchus romeri *(above), from the Early Permian of Texas, USA. This solidly built foot had five short toes, each armed with a long claw. The skull (right) had a curious snout, which looks as if it has been pulled forwards at the top. The teeth were sharp, as in* Aerosaurus *(opposite), but rather more peg-like, and it is almost certain that* Cotylorhynchus *fed on plants. The skull was equivalent in size to that of a sheep, while the body was on the scale of a rhino – a very strange mismatch of sizes!*

THE GEOLOGICAL TIME SCALE

The entire span of geological time is represented as a long ribbon, starting with the origin of the Earth 4,600 million years ago, and documenting major biological events since then. Life arose some 3,500 million years ago; complex life about 1,000 million years ago; and familiar shelled sea animals about 570 million years ago. The pace of change continued slowly, with the oldest fishes dating back to 510 million years, the first land amphibians 380 million years, the oldest reptiles 350 million years, with the mammal-like reptiles emerging 300 million years ago.

True mammals came on the scene 210 million years ago, but spread and diversified only 65 million years ago, after the extinction of the dinosaurs. Humans date from a mere five million years ago. Mammalian evolution, then, seems to be almost an afterthought, tagged on to the end of Earth's history, and a mere four per cent of the whole span. Humans have existed for only 0.1 per cent of the history of our planet.

The geological time scale was devised over years of study, estimating the relative ages of fossil-bearing rocks throughout the world. The "exact" ages in millions of years are based on radiometric dating, by measuring amounts of radioactive decay in various chemical elements in the rocks.

The ribbon diagram (right) represents the entire history of the Earth, showing the dates of some major events, and cartoon indications of the major changes in the physical structure of the Earth and in life upon it.

The first 4000 million years of the Earth's history may seem to be rather devoid of action. Indeed, this first span of time, termed the Precambrian, had for a long time been thought to have lacked all evidences of life. Fossils from this period are still very rare and often hard to interpret. However, biologically, many of the key stages in the evolution of life took place during this interval: the origin of life 3500 million years ago, the origin of more complex-celled life about 2000 million years ago, and multi-celled plants 1000 million years ago. Finally, various worm-like and coral-like creatures are well represented from 650-700 million years ago.

The second great phase of Earth history began 570-600 million years ago, depending upon the time scale used: this was the Phanerozoic, the time of "abundant life". Suddenly, fossils become common in the rocks. Whether or not this is a real indication or a burst of evolution is not clear: all the new creatures have hard shells – shellfish, ancestors of crabs and insects, and the like. Soft-bodied animals may have existed commonly before, but were not often preserved as fossils.

The vertebrate story begins here too, representing only the last half-loop of the time ribbon, and hence about one-ninth of the entire history of the Earth. Small knife-like fishes swam in the seas 510 million years ago. More modern-seeming fishes arose 400 million years ago, and from some of these – the air-breathing fishes – arose the amphibians about 380 million years ago. Vertebrates conquered the land in the course of the next 150 million years, which saw the origin of the reptiles, and their radiation into three major groups: one leading to the turtles, one to the lizards, crocodiles and birds, and one to the mammals.

The mammal-like reptiles were the dominant land vertebrates for 80 million years, until about 225 million years ago, when the dinosaurs took over. The mammals proper, with hair, full warm-bloodedness, and parental care, arose soon after the dinosaurs, about 210 million years ago. However, these first mammals could never become large because of the dominance of the dinosaurs for the next 150 million years.

Finally, 65 million years ago, the dinosaurs, and other land and air reptiles died out in a great extinction event, and the mammals had their chance. A panoply of typical fossil mammals of these 65 million years is shown in expanded form below. Note how small a fraction of the entire history of the Earth is represented by the Age of the Mammals in which we now live.

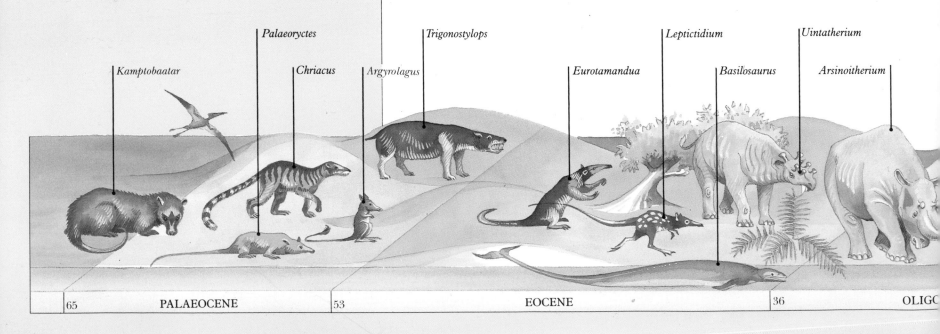

| 65 | PALAEOCENE | 53 | EOCENE | 36 | OLIGO |

505
438 408 360   286 245 208   144   65   present day
500

1,640   1,070

2,780   2,210

3,920   3,350

4,600   1,490 million years ago

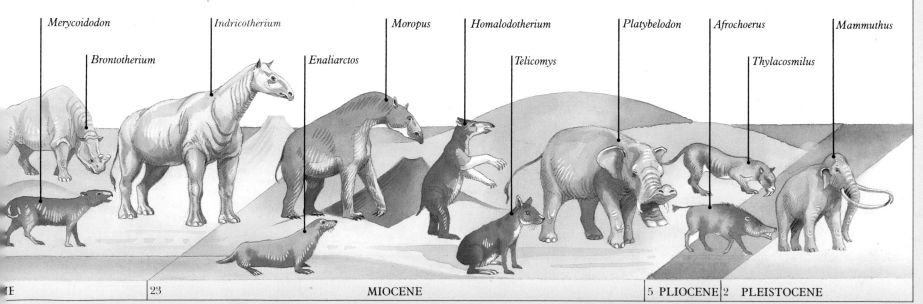

Merycoidodon   *Indricotherium*   *Moropus*   *Homalodotherium*   *Platybelodon*   *Afrochoerus*   *Mammuthus*

Brontotherium   *Enaliarctos*   *Telicomys*   *Thylacosmilus*

E   23   MIOCENE   5 PLIOCENE 2 PLEISTOCENE

pattern of advance. During the course of their evolution, the synapsids included many side branches which were highly successful in their day but did not lead on to further evolutionary stages.

We must always bear in mind that we are looking at evolution backwards, with the benefit of hindsight. We know now that the mammal-like reptiles of the Permian were on the line to the mammals, but evolution could just have easily followed a very different route, and mammals might never have arisen. For example, the Earth might now be full of sail-backed animals, descendants of *Dimetrodon*! It is important to remember that these various groups of prehistoric animals were successful in their day: if they had not been, they could not have survived and left an abundant fossil record. It is also pertinent to note that evolutionary "progress" is not always progress in a human sense, but it can merely be change without improvement.

Indeed, the dominant synapsids of Late Permian times were not on the line to mammals at all. There were three chief groups.

The dinocephalians were part of a major evolutionary

Along the mammal road

The pelycosaurs disappeared by mid Permian times, giving rise to the second wave of synapsid evolution, the therapsids. These animals are known from all continents, and they certainly dominated terrestrial life during the Late Permian period (258–245 million years ago), and during much of the Triassic (245-208 million years ago). It is worth mentioning the main therapsid groups because of their paleoecological importance.

Therapsids showed a variety of advances towards the full mammalian condition. Indeed, such advances had begun already in the pelycosaurs, and it is possible to trace a chain of 20 or 30 evolutionary steps that took place during the Permian and Triassic periods, on the way from a "typical reptile" to a "typical mammal". For example, an advanced pelycosaur like *Dimetrodon* had fewer teeth, specialized canine teeth, and changes to mammal-like bones in the lower jaw and hip region. The first therapsids, only a few million years later, have an enlarged temporal opening, an even more mammal-like lower jaw and jaw hinge, and mammal-like limbs.

It is easy, in retrospect, to discover these seemingly progressive characters that appeared one by one during the evolution of the synapsids. There seems to be a complete series of "missing links" between the primitive reptiles and the first mammals. However, this was not a pre-ordained

The most famous pelycosaur, the sail-backed, mammal-like reptile Dimetrodon limbatus *(above), from the Belle Plains Formation (Early Permian) of Texas, USA. Each enormously elongated bony spine grew out from one of the vertebrae (spinal bones). In life, these supported a "sail" of skin, which probably assisted the animal's temperature control.*

A top view of the skull of the dicynodont mammal-like reptile Oudenodon *(right), from the Teekloof Formation (Late Permian) of the Karoo Basin, South Africa. This plant-eater had powerful jaw muscles which bulged into the great basin-like areas at the back of the skull (top). Below these lie the large round eye sockets and narrow snout.*

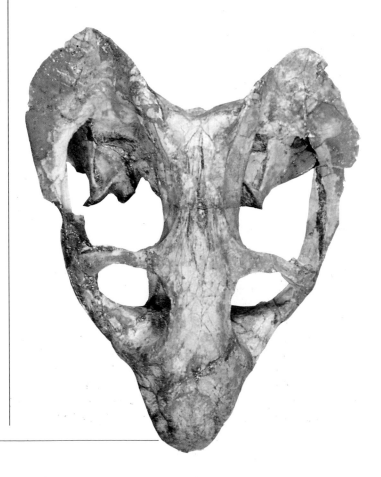

burst that threw up both carnivorous and herbivorous branches. The carnivorous titanosuchians were long, low animals with dog-like skulls, which fed on smaller reptiles and amphibians. The herbivorous tapinocephalians often reached very large size, being 2–3 metres (7–10 feet) long and massively built. *Moschops* was a tapinocephalian with massive limbs and powerful shoulders. Its skull was heavily thickened on top, and it seems that it engaged in head-butting contests with its rivals, just as wild sheep and goats do today.

The gorgonopsians were major carnivores in the Late Permian, known from numerous skeletons from the USSR and South Africa. These hefty and agile predators had massive canine teeth and they could open their jaws very wide in order to expose these teeth. The gorgonopsians presumably hunted the large, thick-skinned tapinocephalians, killing them with powerful stabs of the canine teeth to the neck or belly region, rather like the sabre-toothed cats much later (see page 67).

The third major therapsid group in the Late Permian were the dicynodonts, a group of 50 or so species that ranged in size from a small cat to a rhinoceros. These herbivores had almost turtle-like faces: they had lost most or all of their teeth, and cut up their plant food with sharp horn-covered jaw edges. The dicynodonts were hugely successful, occupying most herbivorous ways of life over

A skull of the therocephalian mammal-like reptile Zinnosaurus, discovered recently in the Late Permian sediments of the Karoo Basin, South Africa. The therocephalians were small to moderate-sized carnivores with dog-like skulls. The teeth included sharp incisors and long canines, but these have broken off in this specimen.

much of the world, and yet they were nearly wiped out at the end of the Permian period.

The mass death

The largest mass extinction of all time happened at the end of the Permian period, 245 million years ago. In the seas, many groups of shellfish, corals, fishes and other animals disappeared, apparently within a short time. On land, the mammal-like reptiles and several other reptile groups were hit hard. The dinocephalians and gorgonopsians disappeared completely, and the dicynodonts were nearly wiped out.

The causes of this mass extinction are uncertain. Most geologists believe that there were major and relatively sudden changes in the positions of the continents, and that this might have affected animals in shallow seas and on land. During the Permian, the continents were moving together and fusing into the supercontinent known as Pangaea.

Since the beginning of time, it is believed the Earth's crust has been mobile. There has been much debate this century about the theory of continental drift, the idea that the continental land masses have been, and are still, sliding around the globe and moving relative to each other. There is a great deal of evidence for this theory: the coasts of Africa and South America would fit together neatly if the South

(Continued on page 26.)

JAWS, EARS AND TEETH, AND THE ORIGIN OF MAMMALS

What is a mammal? There is no doubt today about the answer. A mammal is distinguished from a reptile by the possession of hair rather than scales, mammary glands to suckle the young on milk, and full ectothermy or "warm-bloodedness". However, the dividing line is less clear when dealing with fossils. A long series of fossil forms, the mammal-like reptiles, document the acquisition of mammalian characters over a time span of some 100 million years.

The distinction between mammal and reptile in terms of fossils may seem rather arbitrary, since it is not the same as for living forms. Of necessity it relies on bones and teeth, specifically minor features of the jaw joint and the shapes of certain teeth. However, the jaw character in particular is crucial: there was a switch from one jaw hinge to another, and a shift of the reptilian jaw joint into the mammalian middle ear. This remarkable story is contained in detail in the fossil record, in a sequence of extremely well-preserved skulls.

The animals involved in the story of mammalian jaw evolution vary greatly in size, but the thread of change is clear. The largest is the primitive pelycosaur **Dimetrodon** (1), *followed by the next in the sequence,* **Thrinaxodon** (2), *and* **Morganucodon** (3), *a tiny shrew-sized animal.*

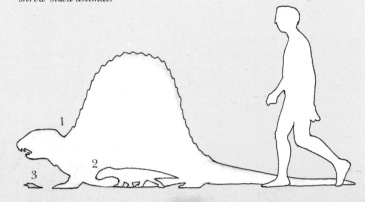

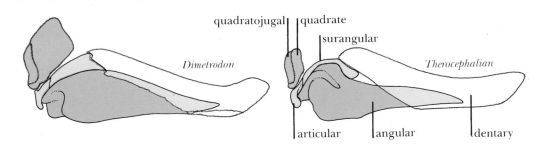

The evolution of the reptilian jaw joint to the mammalian middle ear bones is shown in the sequence of six jaws (above). The complex lower jaw of **Dimetrodon** *consisted of numerous bones, with the actual joint between the quadrate and articular bones. Over time, the dentary became the sole lower jaw bone; the quadrate and articular shifted inside the middle ear, to become the tiny ear bones or ossicles known as the hammer and anvil.*

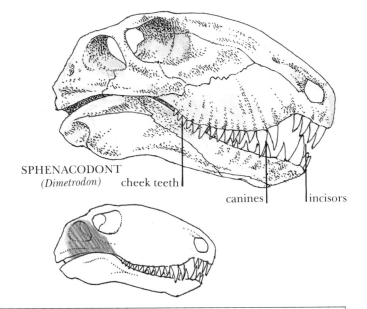

SPHENACODONT
(*Dimetrodon*)   cheek teeth

canines   incisors

The early mammal-like reptiles (above and right) had slightly different-shaped or differentiated teeth – cheek teeth, canines and incisors – although they all still retained a similar basic shape (right).

TEETH

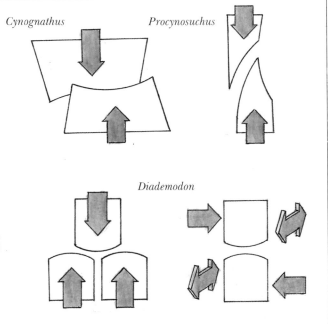

Cynognathus   *Procynosuchus*

Diademodon

Advanced mammal-like reptiles, and then mammals, showed many changes in their teeth, especially in their ability to crush food. The early cynodonts, **Procynosuchus** and **Cynognathus** (*top*), could shear their prey of insects and small vertebrates. In other words, their teeth cut past each other like the blades of a pair of strong shears. The later herbivorous cynodont **Diademodon** (*below*) had an additional ability, namely chewing. The teeth do not meet head on but are offset so that their surfaces alternate; and the jaw action causes back-and-forwards as well as sideways chewing movements.

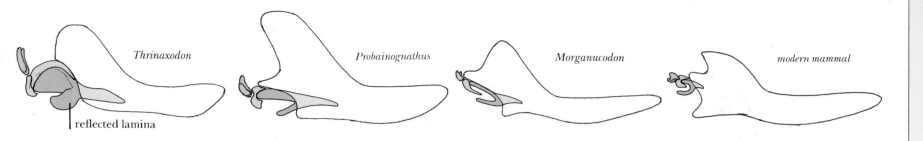

Thrinaxodon   *Probainognathus*   *Morganucodon*   *modern mammal*

reflected lamina

The angular bone (shown in red in the skull sequence above) shifted from forming a major part of the side of the jaw, in the mammal-like reptiles, to become the mammalian ectotympanic bone, a C-shaped support for the eardrum. In most mammal-like reptiles, the angular bore a curved sheet of bone, the reflected lamina, which may have formed an edge to the eardrum in those creatures.

Later mammal-like reptiles, and mammals (right), show more detailed differentiation of the teeth. The main jaw muscle, the masseter, also increased greatly in size.

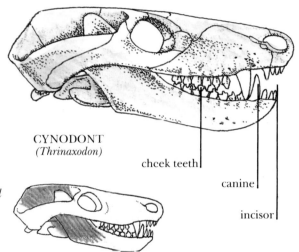

CYNODONT
(Thrinaxodon)

cheek teeth

canine

incisor

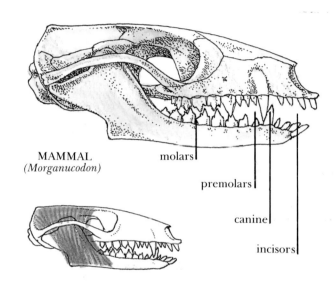

MAMMAL
(Morganucodon)

molars

premolars

canine

incisors

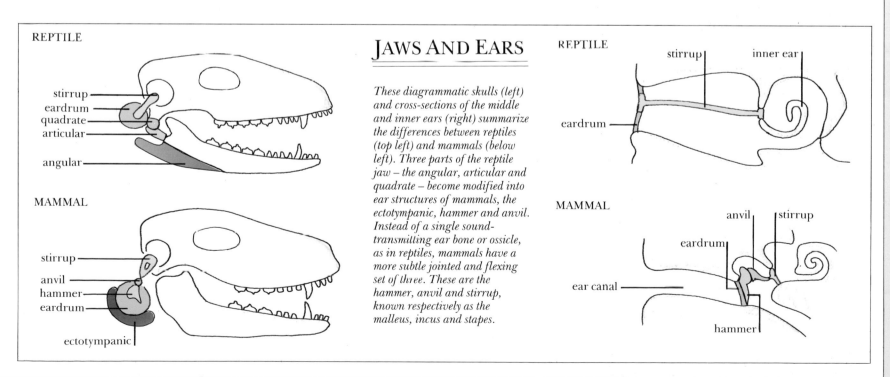

REPTILE

stirrup
eardrum
quadrate
articular

angular

MAMMAL

stirrup
anvil
hammer
eardrum

ectotympanic

JAWS AND EARS

These diagrammatic skulls (left) and cross-sections of the middle and inner ears (right) summarize the differences between reptiles (top left) and mammals (below left). Three parts of the reptile jaw – the angular, articular and quadrate – become modified into ear structures of mammals, the ectotympanic, hammer and anvil. Instead of a single sound-transmitting ear bone or ossicle, as in reptiles, mammals have a more subtle jointed and flexing set of three. These are the hammer, anvil and stirrup, known respectively as the malleus, incus and stapes.

REPTILE

stirrup
inner ear

eardrum

MAMMAL

anvil
stirrup

eardrum

ear canal

hammer

Atlantic Ocean were closed; fossil distributions make sense only if there were once close links between the Americas, Europe, Africa, Antarctica, Australia and Asia; major geological features match closely across today's oceans, and they can best be explained if the continents were in different positions.

It is also easy to explain the great changes in climates which had taken place in geological eras if the continents are returned to their original positions. For example, North America and Europe lay right on the equator in Carboniferous and Permian times, which readily explains the fossil evidence for tropical forests and arid deserts.

The formation of Pangaea in Permian times reduced the numbers of offshore seas, and also affected the interiors of the continents. The different animal groups that were formerly restricted to shallow seas and coastal strips were either "squeezed out" by the fusion of land masses, or brought into contact with other animals that they had never encountered before. This is supposed to have caused a massive extinction, which saw the loss of one-half of all animal families, and as much as nineteen-twentieths of all species.

After the extinction event, whatever may have caused it,

Entwined skeletons of two dicynodont mammal-like reptiles, Lystrosaurus, *from the Beaufort Group (Early Triassic) rocks of South Africa. The skeleton in front lies from left to right and is missing the tail, while the one behind has the head on the right.* Lystrosaurus *marks the recovery of the reptiles from the mass extinction at the end of the Permian period, which nearly drove the mammal-like reptiles to extinction. Only one or two lineages survived, which later evolved into mammals.*

evidence of land animals is remarkably depleted around the world. The early reptiles of the Triassic were dominated to a seemingly preposterous extent by one type of dicynodont, *Lystrosaurus.* It is known from six or more regions worldwide, and in every case it makes up more than nine-tenths of animal remains. This degree of dominance is not at all typical of natural assemblages of animals, and it indicates that there was a great deal of empty "ecospace" that had been cleared out by the extinction. For example, there were no other large herbivores or carnivores in the *Lystrosaurus* records at all.

Clues in the skeleton

During the Triassic period (245–208 million years ago), various new groups of diapsid reptiles became established, and these ultimately came to the fore. However, the dicynodonts also radiated (evolved and diversified rapidly) a second time, to become important medium-sized and large herbivores in many parts of the world. Some smaller synapsids also became re-established, mainly as carnivores, but also, later, as herbivores. The main group of interest here was the cynodonts.

The first cynodont, *Procynosuchus* from the Late Permian of southern Africa, already shows hints of what was to come. This terrier-sized animal was clearly carnivorous, having lines of sharp teeth along its jaws. The limbs seem to have been adapted for running and swimming. However, the skull and skeleton showed some major advances over Permian contemporaries. The braincase was enlarged and the temporal opening formed an open area beside it with a zygomatic arch – the cheekbone arch beneath the eyes which is typical of mammals. The teeth were differentiated into incisors, canines, and cheek teeth, just as in modern mammals, and the numbers of teeth were reduced. The bones of the palate joined in the middle to form a partial secondary palate, the dividing shelf between the nose and mouth, and a feature not seen in earlier synapsids.

The "missing links"

During the Triassic, the cynodonts developed into several families of small and medium-sized carnivores, such as the agile dog-like *Probelesodon* from Brazil, and two families of herbivores. Some of the later members of the group are almost indistinguishable from the first mammals, and

The short-snouted skull of Lystrosaurus *(above), showing the pair of canine teeth and the sharp, bony jaw edges. The herbivorous dicynodonts had lost most of their teeth, as did turtles and birds, yet all were still able to feed efficiently on tough plant food. The large round openings on the top of the skull are the eye sockets, and a large nostril is halfway up the snout.*

A partial skull and skeleton of the oldest cynodont, Procynosuchus *(left), from the Late Permian deposits of South Africa. Cynodonts were a group of advanced, carnivorous mammal-like reptiles that arose in the Late Permian; they nearly disappeared in the end-of-Permian mass extinction event, but recovered to evolve widely in the Triassic period. They included the direct ancestors of the mammals.*

PROBELESODON

The later cynodonts probably looked so much like mammals that if they lived today, it would be hard to call them reptiles. There is clear evidence that the later mammal-like reptiles such as Probelesodon *had hair and warm blood: the bones of the snout region show tiny pits for the nerves and blood vessels that served sensory whiskers. If they had whiskers, they probably had normal body hair as well.*

indeed the first mammals are defined on an apparently minor change in the nature of the jaw joint.

There are still problems in establishing the relationships of the cynodonts to the transition from reptile to mammal, partly because of the number of evolutionary changes taking place, and also because of the relative abundance of animal fossils close to the transition. This is a very different situation from the more celebrated change from reptile to bird, where *Archaeopteryx* is our sole "missing link". For the origin of mammals we have too many "missing links", spaced very closely in time and relationships, and it is hard to disentangle them.

Nevertheless, the generally accepted characters that distinguish mammal from reptile are that the jaw joint shifted from one position to another, and that the old jaw joint was still there – but inside the ear (see pages 24-25).

The key to success

One of the mammals' keys to success is often said to reside in their teeth. It is true that mammals have been much more adaptable and successful in their range of diet than any other amniote group. The most important

feature of mammalian teeth is occlusion – the fact that our cheek teeth, the molars and premolars, meet face to face and grind over each other. Mammals can chew, something that no other animals can do. Herbivorous reptiles and birds swallow their food in chunks, and it has to be ground up in a specialized stomach structure, called a gizzard in birds, which is full of grit or small stones which do the grinding.

The earliest incidence of tooth occlusion is seen in herbivorous cynodonts of the Middle Triassic, such as *Diademodon* from South America, where the narrow lower teeth come together with the broader upper teeth. During the jaw-closing cycle the teeth met, and then the lower jaw pulled back a little. This allowed much more efficient tearing of food than in the standard reptilian system, seen in earlier cynodonts, where the cheek teeth did not meet face to face, but merely cut past each other like the blades of a pair of scissors. Instead of each cheek tooth producing a single small tear, the cheek teeth working together in *Diademodon* would have produced a large tear.

Later relatives of *Diademodon* had cheek teeth with numerous cusps and facets, the points and valleys that we have on our molars and premolars. During feeding, the jaw cycle ended with a pronounced backwards pull of the lower jaw, and all six or seven lower jaw molars were pulled back in a single powerful movement to tear a piece of leaf or stem into tiny fragments. As the jaw movement ended, the molars met tightly, and any remaining plant fragments would have been effectively crushed.

New teeth for old

Related to occlusion of the teeth in advanced cynodonts, and in mammals, is the question of tooth replacement. We are used to the idea that we have only two sets of teeth throughout our lives: the milk teeth up to about the age of seven or eight, and the adult teeth after that. This is related to the increase in the size of our mouths during growth. Some rare people have a third set of teeth that may come during their twenties, and there are clearly advantages in having further sets like this, not least in reducing dentists' bills! Yet mammals are the exception. All other vertebrates have numerous sets of teeth during their lives.

In fishes, amphibians and reptiles, teeth are replaced continuously. New ones appear as old ones become worn and fall out. The change to having only two sets seems to have taken place by the Early or Middle Triassic, in cynodonts such as *Thrinaxodon* and *Diademodon*. This probably occurred because of the complexity of their

The fossil skull of Cynognathus craternonotus *(right) from the Early Triassic of the Karoo Basin, South Africa. The long canine tooth has small, sharp incisors in front, and broader cheek teeth behind. These cheek teeth tore the meat from the bones of prey animals.*

The skeleton of Diademodon *(above), a small herbivore from the Early Triassic of South Africa (see also page 24). The skull is broad, with large openings at the back which were associated with powerful jaw muscles. The animal is curled up, a common position of preservation; it may have died in its sleep, or perhaps its body was swept into this position after death.*

tooth occlusion, and the need to maintain precise tooth-tooth contact for efficient chewing. The system would not have worked if teeth were forever falling out and new ones were popping up in their place.

The last cynodonts, the tritheledonts and tritylodonts, showed this advanced tooth occlusion, as well as other mammalian characters. Most experts agree that they were not quite mammals, although they probably looked very like mammals from the outside. They still retained the reptilian articular-quadrate jaw joint, but elsewhere in the skull and skeleton they are mammalian.

The tritheledonts are known only from a few jaw fragments and partial skulls as fossils in Late Triassic and Early Jurassic rocks, but these show a very mammal-like zygomatic arch and the loss of the bar of bone separating the eye orbit and temporal opening.

The tritylodonts are much better known, being represented by skulls and skeletons from many parts of the world in rocks of Early and Middle Jurassic age (208–163 million years ago). These were successful herbivores with superficially rodent-like skulls. On each side of the jaw there were two or three incisor teeth, one of which was elongated, rather like that of a rat or a rabbit, and six to eight square cheek teeth in straight rows. The upper molars bore three longitudinal rows of crescent-shaped cusps, while the lower molars had two rows. When the jaws moved back and forwards, the rows of cusps slid between each other and must have ground up tough stems with the efficiency of two cheese graters rubbing together.

Standing upright

The skeletons of these later tritylodonts are also well known, and show major advantages. As with earlier cynodonts, the limbs hold the body up in an essentially erect or upright posture. Primitive reptiles, and indeed most living reptiles, have sprawling limbs in which the elbows and knees stick out sideways, and the stride consists of an inefficient sideways sweep. By Middle Triassic times, the cynodonts had an erect hindlimb which was tucked beneath the hip girdle, as in modern mammals, and which swung back and forwards. The erect posture and gait is believed to be more efficient than the sprawling version, since less energy is used in supporting the weight of the body, and also it lengthens the stride.

SKULL EVOLUTION

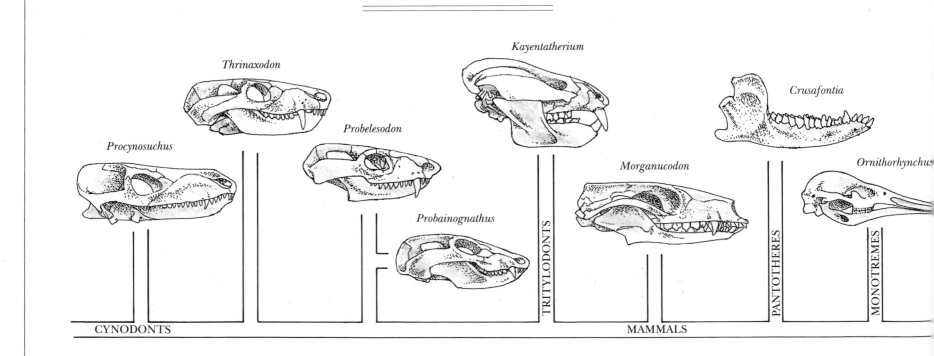

Thrinaxodon

Procynosuchus

Probelesodon

Kayentatherium

Crusafontia

Probainognathus

Morganucodon

Ornithorhynchus

CYNODONTS

TRITYLODONTS

MAMMALS

PANTOTHERES

MONOTREMES

A skull of the tritylodont Bienotherium yunnanense *from the Lufeng Series (Early Jurassic) rocks of Yunnan, China. The tritylodonts were small, advanced mammal-like reptiles that lived on through the origin of the mammals, into the Jurassic. The skull is very like that of a small rat, and it is likely that tritylodonts were specialized gnawing animals. In this specimen, the original bone is brown; the missing portions have been restored in white plaster, based on other tritylodont skulls.*

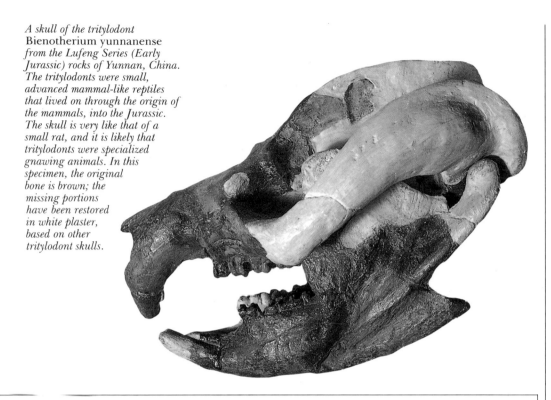

The evolution of the mammals, from their immediate ancestors the cynodonts, is illustrated by the changes to the skulls shown here in sequence. The teeth gradually became more and more differentiated into incisors, canines and molar cheek teeth. The jaw joint shifted (see pages 24–25), and the eye socket amalgamated with the opening behind it, in the cheek region.

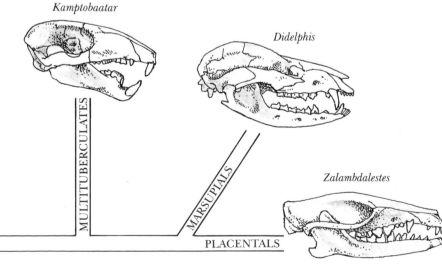

Kamptobaatar

Didelphis

Zalambdalestes

MULTITUBERCULATES

MARSUPIALS

PLACENTALS

Decline of the mammals

There were two major extinctions during the Late Triassic, one 225 million years ago and the other 208 million years ago, right at the end of the period. The dicynodonts and other important groups died out during the first, and the second wiped out further families. The dinosaurs had arisen from their diapsid predecessors by the end of the Middle Triassic, some 230 million years ago, and it seems that they evolved rapidly after both of the extinction events. This opportunistic filling of roles left vacant matches what happened at the beginning of the Triassic, after the end-Permian mass extinction.

The result of the Late Triassic extinctions was that the synapsids were dealt a blow from which they barely recovered. Only three families of small animals survived: the trithcledonts, tritylodonts and earliest mammals. The first two had died out by Middle Jurassic times, leaving only the rare mammals to live on through the long Age of the Dinosaurs, a span of 160 million years.

This curious hiatus between the rule of the mammal-like reptiles, and the later rise of the true mammals, is sobering when we wish to argue how wonderfully well adapted mammals are, or how unsuccessful the dinosaurs were. The dinosaurs and the mammals appeared around the same time, though perhaps with the dinosaurs some 10–15 million years earlier; yet it was the dinosaurs that ruled the Earth for 160 million years. These great reptiles held back the mammals.

The first mammal

The first mammals appeared in the Late Triassic period – and the earliest dated finds are only odd teeth. The first reasonably complete remains are those of *Morganucodon*, a small weasel-like animal found fossilized in caves in South Wales and the Bristol region of south-western England. Many small animals were washed in or became trapped when they fell into the cracks and crevices. Because the carcasses were generally left undisturbed by scavengers, they are often beautifully preserved. The Welsh and Bristol remains have yielded rich finds of lizard-like sphenodontians, tritylodonts, small dinosaurs and the treasured *Morganucodon*.

A great deal is known about this tiny 2–3 centimetres (1 inch) long creature. But how can this be when all that remains are fossilized teeth and bones alone?

Firstly, these earliest of mammals were similar in size and adaptations to living insectivorous mammals. But more importantly, there are some specific clues in the

skeleton. There is a complete secondary palate, a structure separating the nose from the mouth, first seen in early cynodonts (see page 27). This shows that *Morganucodon* could breathe and feed at the same time, as can modern mammals, but not most modern reptiles. Taking in large amounts of food is a requirement for endothermy or "warm-bloodedness", where energy is being used at a fast rate to create heat. The advanced teeth allowed *Morganucodon* to process its food rapidly and efficiently, and it also had a complete covering of insulating hair (fur). The hair itself is not fossilized, but *Morganucodon* has many small openings in the snout bones, through which we believe that nerves and blood vessels passed to a set of sensory whiskers. Whiskers are used to detect movements nearby, and to hunt small prey – but they are made from modified hairs. Whiskers could therefore have arisen only if *Morganucodon* had hair. If it had hair, it insulated the body and is an essential corollary of full-scale endothermy.

Mammals and milk

Paleontologists conclude that *Morganucodon* was nocturnal because its skull shows very large eye sockets, indicating big eyes which would be necessary for seeing in the dark. The brain shows expanded visual and auditory areas, as well. We know this because the bones are so well preserved that it has been possible to make accurate internal casts of the actual shape of the soft brain, and the different sensory regions can be distinguished. Good eyesight and hearing are present in nocturnal animals today, and most living mammalian insectivores are nocturnal. The nocturnal lifestyle seems typical of most early mammals, and it makes sense in a world dominated

Cromhall Quarry (above), one of the famous Bristol "fissure sites" in southwest England, yielded some of the oldest known mammal fossils. The reddish sediment, dated as Late Triassic in age, once formed the floor of a cave, having been washed into a deep crevice or fissure in the ancient limestone surface, some 210 million years ago. Small reptiles, beetles and mammals

fell down these fissures and were trapped. Some may have survived for a time in the caves, but they were eventually entombed, rendering tiny yet exquisitely preserved bones and body cases for study today.

The tiny skull of Erythrotherium, *a morganucodontid from the Early Jurassic – one of the oldest known mammals (right). This skull is only a few millimetres long, and it shows in excellent detail the sharp teeth that were used for crushing the hard body cases of insects. The larger teeth had two roots passing into the bone.*

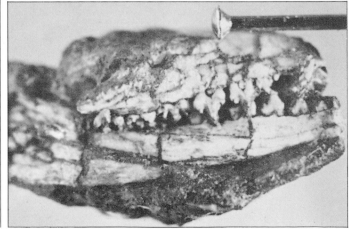

MEGAZOSTRODON

The oldest well-known mammal, this morganucodontid from the Early Jurassic of South Africa was a tiny, shrew-sized animal that hunted insects in the undergrowth at night. It was dwarfed by the dinosaurs, the dominant animals of the day. Here a startled Megazostrodon *surveys the scene from the footprint of a prosauropod dinosaur.*

by highly succesful reptiles such as dinosaurs and flying pterosaurs, which hunted by day.

Did female *Morganucodon* have mammary glands and feed its young on milk? The name "mammal" derives from the same word as "mammary", and the ability to suckle young is often regarded as a key mammalian attribute. Again, such soft parts cannot be fossilized, but there are two lines of supporting evidence. Most important is the dental condition of *Morganucodon*. Careful dissection of the fossil jaws, and comparisons of skulls of different sizes, has shown that *Morganucodon* had two sets of teeth in its lifetime. Mammals today are mostly born without teeth, and the milk teeth appear only towards the end of the suckling period. The same seems to have been true of *Morganucodon*. If this first mammal had not suckled its young, they would have required teeth early on, in order to feed on solid food.

The second argument for mammary glands is less clear. These glands are formed from modified sweat glands in the skin. Since *Morganucodon* was an endotherm, it must have had sweat glands, in order to dissipate excess heat, and such structures must have been present in cynodonts back to *Thrinaxodon*, at least. Therefore, there had been plenty of time for mammary glands to evolve.

The long twilight of the mammals

It is difficult to reconstruct the details of early mammalian evolution. Although the Jurassic and Cretaceous periods (208–66 million years ago) represent three-quarters of the evolution of the group, there are very few fossils, and most are fragmentary. We are extremely lucky that *Morganucodon*, the first mammal, is so completely known. When George Gaylord Simpson, the distinguished North

(Continued on page 36.)

LATE CRETACEOUS MAMMALS OF MONGOLIA

Most mammals from the Mesozoic era, which represented the first two-thirds of mammalian history, are known from isolated and often incomplete remains. The Late Cretaceous dinosaur beds of Mongolia have been a treasure trove of early mammal specimens since their discovery in the 1960s. Expeditions from the USSR, and especially from Poland, continue to uncover complete skeletons of tiny mammals.

The main groups represented are the multituberculates, tree-living herbivores such as *Kamptobaatar* at the top left; the placentals, such as *Zalambdalestes* at the bottom left; and the marsupials, such as *Deltatheridium* at the bottom right.

The world as it was then.

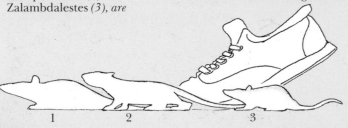

Late Cretaceous mammals were very small, on the same scale as shrews and mice. All three shown here, Deltatheridium *(1),* Kamptobaatar *(2) and* Zalambdalestes *(3), are dwarfed by a human foot. In their day, they would be almost insignificant compared to tyrannosaur dinosaurs such as* Tarbosaurus *in the background.*

1   2   3

CRUSAFONTIA

Jurassic mammals such as the pantothere Crusafontia, *from the Guimarota mine in Portugal, were tiny insectivores. The bones of this remarkable specimen were almost perfectly preserved in a coal sediment, which has been painstakingly removed in its entirety. The coal was cleared from one side of the skeleton; this was embedded in clear resin, and the coal was then cleared from the other side.*

American mammal paleontologist, reviewed mammals from these times, in 1927, he stated that all known specimens could be placed in a hat. More remains have come to light since then, but the whole lot could still fit into a larger top hat. This is a hopelessly poor fossil record when it is compared with the hundreds of tonnes of mammal bones known from the last 65 million years!

The fossils do indicate some ten or so main lineages of mammalian evolution during the Jurassic and Cretaceous, even if some of these are represented only by single jaws or other scraps. Apart from the mor-

ganucodontids, one or two incomplete fossils of different mammals are known from the Early and Middle Jurassic, but then there is a long gap until Late Jurassic times (163–144 million years ago) when as many as eight mammalian lineages have been identified. Most of the Late Jurassic mammals are known only from jaws and teeth, but these remains are sufficient to determine their broad relationships. Teeth are regarded as very important by paleontologists since they show so much variation between different forms, and because they are the hardest parts of the skeleton, and hence the most easily fossilized.

Unusually complete

The Late Jurassic dryolestid mammal *Crusafontia* is unusual in being known from a nearly complete skeleton, found in exceptionally rich fossil deposits in Portugal. This recently-found specimen shows an animal about 20 centimetres (8 inches) long, which probably looked rather like a tree shrew. It shows a variety of adaptations for living in trees, leaping from branch to branch, and feeding on a variety of insects and fruit.

The most important group that arose in the Late Jurassic was the multituberculates. They survived for 130 million years into the Oligocene epoch (about 30 million years ago), well after the extinction of all other primitive mammal groups.

Complete skeletons of multituberculates are known, such as *Kamptobaatar* from the Late Cretaceous of Mongolia, and *Ptilodus* from the Palaeocene of Canada. They suggest arboreal habits: there is a long prehensile tail which could have been used for grasping branches, and a reversible foot (as in squirrels) which allows them to walk up or down a tree trunk. There is even a pair of small bones in the lower belly region, the "marsupial bones", which show that multituberculates had pouches for their developing young, as marsupials do today.

The remarkable skeleton of Crusafontia *(see opposite). The jaws are at the bottom left, a chunk of backbone lies across the middle top, with two hind limbs symmetrically on either side at the right. The skeleton has been artificially embedded in clear resin.*

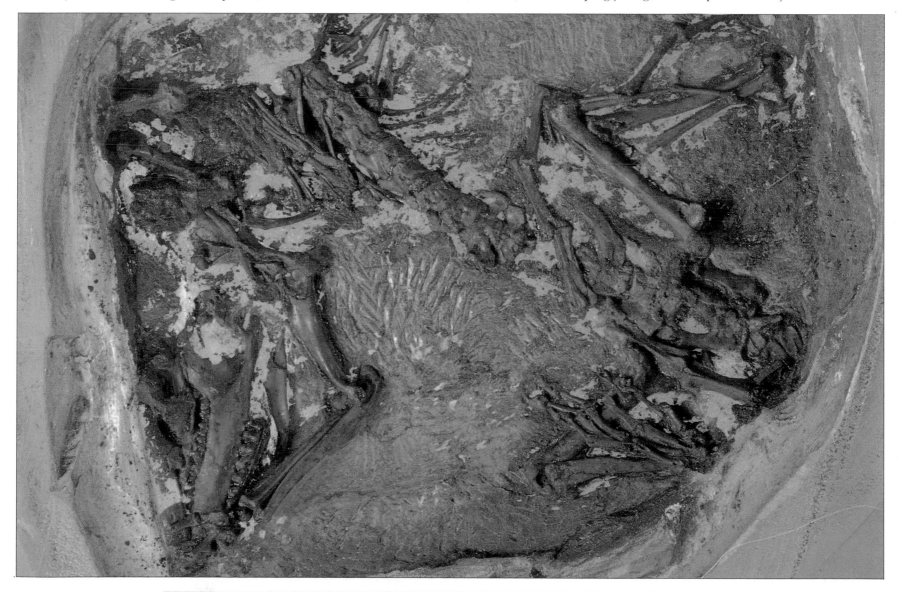

The fossil skeleton of Ptilodus, *a multituberculate from the Late Palaeocene rocks of the Crazy Mountain Basin, Montana, USA (see page 44). The preserved bone is black against a background of light-coloured mudstone. The skull is rather broken, the bones of the trunk are jumbled, and the tail curves round on the right, between the hind legs.*

The modern groups appear

There were a dozen or more groups of Mesozoic mammals during the Age of Dinosaurs, most of which lived for only relatively short spans during the Jurassic and Cretaceous periods. Only the multituberculates outlasted the others. Modern mammals fall into three different but closely-related groups: monotremes, marsupials and placentals. These three are divided by their methods of reproduction, and their relative size and importance today increases from the first to the last noted.

Only two types of monotreme still survive – the duck-billed platypus and echidna of Australasia. They lay eggs. The young hatch out in a fairly undeveloped stage, and they move to a fold of skin in the belly region of the mother, where they suckle on rather primitive nipples which are midway between sweat glands and fully-developed mammary glands. The living monotremes are both rather specialized, the platypus dabbling for freshwater worms and shellfish with its duck bill, and the echidna using its tubular snout for catching insects. Both are toothless as adults, but the juvenile platypus has a set of peculiar molar teeth which are soon lost.

Pouches and placentas

The marsupials and placentals arose during the Early Cretaceous, at the time predicted from the evolutionary diagram, since these two are more closely related to each other than either is to the monotremes. Living marsupials, such as kangaroos, opossums and koalas, are typical of Australasia, but also of South America. They go one step further than the monotremes in not laying an egg, but the young is born tiny and undeveloped, and it drags itself into a special incubating pouch where it suckles for some time before venturing forth.

Marsupials seem to have arisen in North or South America, which is where their oldest fossils occur. These fossils are jaws and teeth, and they can be identified as marsupial because they have three premolars and four molars, while placentals have four or five premolars and three molars. The mammalian remains of the Late Cretaceous (70 million years ago) of North and South America are dominated by marsupials, containing representatives of three families. Two of these three were wiped out at the end of the Cretaceous, the third going on to found the marsupial dynasties in South America and Australia (see chapter four). It is interesting to speculate what might have happened if all three marsupial families had survived the mass extinction: would we now have a world dominated by marsupials?

The dominant mammals today are the placentals. They retain their young inside until a late stage of development, nourishing them in the womb via the placenta, an organ specialized for transfer of nutrients between the mother's blood and the baby's blood. Placentals are represented by seven or eight families in the Late Cretaceous in various parts of the world. The remains from Mongolia are best, where animals like *Zalambdalestes* and *Barunlestes* lived side by side with the multituberculate *Kamptobaatar* and the enigmatic *Deltatheridium*, which may have been a marsupial, or placental, or neither. *Zalambdalestes* was an agile hedgehog-sized animal that fed on insects by night. The brain was relatively small, but the olfactory area was enlarged, indicating a good sense of smell. The limbs were advanced in comparison with *Megazostrodon*, being fully erect in posture, and the hind limbs were long and strong enough to suggest that *Zalambdalestes* jumped like a rabbit.

The death of the dinosaurs

The mass extinction at the end of the Cretaceous period, 65 million years ago, is often known as the Cretaceous-Tertiary or K-T event. It is the most famous mass extinction of all time. On land, the main group to disappear were the dinosaurs, and that is reason enough why the event is so celebrated. But it also saw the end of the flying pterosaurs, two families of marsupials, and a few others. Yet it had little

Prospecting for bones in the Late Cretaceous sediments of the Gobi Desert, Mongolia. Teams of paleontologists from the USSR and Poland have explored these inhospitable areas since the early 1960s. They have collected large numbers of dinosaur specimens, as well as the finest fossils of Mesozoic mammals. There is no short cut: still the best way to find good specimens is to spend hours walking back and forwards, with your eyes close to the ground.

effect on frogs, lizards, snakes, crocodilians, turtles, birds and placental mammals.

There is still intense debate both about *what* happened, and *why*. We still cannot answer either question clearly. At least one can say, in answer to the "what", that certain groups went and others did not; but there is no clear taxonomic or ecological pattern to the losers and the survivors. It cannot be said, however, how long it all took: one day or ten million years. The evidence at present suggests that half of the groups which eventually died out were already in long-term decline, while the others genuinely seem to have gone "out with a bang".

Whatever its cause, the K-T event was the trigger for the beginning of the Age of the Mammals – our present age. It cleared the stocks and left the way open for mammals to show their true potential, after 160 million years of living in the shadow of the dinosaurs.

CHAPTER TWO

INTO THE LIGHT

After the extinction of the dinosaurs, the placental mammals developed extensively and rapidly in most parts of the world. Within ten million years, nearly all the modern placental groups had appeared – mammals as diverse as horses and bats, hedgehogs and whales. This spectacular burst of evolution is known as an adaptive radiation, and gave rise to a diverse array of new mammalian forms, some familiar to us, but many strange and unfamiliar, even bizarre. These animals are particularly well known from fossils of the Palaeocene and Eocene epochs in North America and Europe.

Filling the empty landscape

The world of the Early Palaeocene epoch, 65–63 million years ago, was nearly as empty of life on land as it had been at the start of the Triassic period, some 180 million years before (see page 16). Nearly all medium-sized and large animals including dinosaurs, pterosaurs and certain crocodilians, had been wiped out by the K-T extinction event. The smaller frogs, salamanders, lizards, snakes, turtles and other crocodilians continued unaffected, but their lives were specialized and mostly inconspicuous. Birds still had an important role, but there were almost no animals larger than a cat living and feeding in the lush forests, on the ground or in the trees. Some very large crocodilians did survive the K-T event, but these presumably stayed close to water.

In many ways, the wildlife was probably rather similar to urbanized Europe or North America today, minus the human beings and domestic animals. There were no

The fossil bat Archaeonycteris *from the Eocene deposits of the Messel pit, near Frankfurt, Germany. The preservation is so good because of the unusual conditions of fossilization. The carcass fell to the bottom of a lake and was buried under fine mud, in oxygen-free conditions. In the absence of oxygen, normal decay cannot take place; and scavengers, which would normally dismember and damage the body, are kept at bay. The bat's long arms and thin fingers, which support the wing membranes, are clearly visible on either side. The hind limbs are drawn up so that the feet touch in the midline.*

medium- or large-sized animals, but probably plenty of smaller reptiles and birds, and a few small mammals that crept out at night.

Surviving the mass extinction

The adaptive radiation of placental mammals during the Palaeocene and Early Eocene (65–52 million years) has often been seen as proof of their great evolutionary potential and advanced characters. We are placental mammals, and of course we find it easy to list all our advantages in comparison with "lesser" vertebrates: large brain, intense parental care, endothermy or warm-bloodedness, adaptable diet and so on. However, placental mammals evolved and diversified only after a mass extinction event, whatever its cause, had cleared out the previously dominant groups. They survived this extinction event perhaps by chance, and they were the first to become successful. It was an opportunistic move on their part.

It could be argued that placental mammals were progressive in the sense that they weathered the crisis and then underwent adaptive radiation. There are two aspects to consider if we wish to propose that the placentals proved their superiority during these times. One: did they survive the K-T extinction because of superior adaptations lacked by the dinosaurs, pterosaurs and other groups? Two: did they evolve first in the Palaeocene, ahead of other surviving groups, because of superior adaptations?

The first question, concerning who survives and who fails in mass extinctions, generally turns out to favour a hypothesis of chance rather than good adaptation. Detailed studies of particular mass extinctions, and

statistical analyses of all known extinction events, have turned up only very limited evidence of selection. In other words, it has proved very hard to find any particular factor conferring success or failure during mass extinctions. The best evidence to date suggests that those animals which had very wide distributions over the Earth stood a better chance of surviving than those that did not. There is no evidence that good adaptation, high intelligence or biochemical efficiency are advantageous during such great crises.

This relatively new notion, based on a variety of studies in large-scale evolution or macroevolution, can be summed up in two slogans. Firstly, survival during mass extinctions depends on "good luck rather than good genes". Secondly, mass extinctions "reset the evolutionary rules".

The first phrase has already been explained, but the second has deeper implications. It involves the suggestion that normal Darwinian evolution, known variously as natural selection, "survival of the fittest" and so on, is the key to evolution most of the time, but that mass extinctions upset the normal calculations. Survivors and losers of these crises are not the same as the survivors and losers in life's normal evolutionary path. The ability to run faster than your competitor, or to produce more young, count for nothing when the asteroid hits, or when the climate is disturbed dramatically. Hence mass extinctions are said to shake up the system, to reset it. Nature only returns to normal some ten million years or so after the event, when sudden bursts of adaptive radiation have taken place and restored diversity among plant and animal communities.

The marsupials lose out

In the case of the K-T event – the mass extinction at the end of the Cretaceous period – there was little to choose between marsupial and the placental mammals during the Late Cretaceous. Both groups seemed to be successful in the Americas, where they may have originated. Both were reasonably diverse, although placentals slightly more so than marsupials. However, the marsupials lost two out of three families during the event, while the placentals seem to have lost none. In size and habits the Late Cretaceous mammals from each group show no obvious differences in character, so it would be hard to argue that the decimation of the marsupials was other than bad luck. Indeed, during the succeeding Palaeocene epoch, the marsupials underwent major evolutionary bursts of their own, particularly in South America, where

A field party working in the famous Scarritt Quarry in the Fort Union Formation of the Crazy Mountain Basin. This Late Palaeocene deposit was found by accident by a paleontologist looking for dinosaurs in 1901. Since then, professional collectors have unearthed 79 species of mammals, as well as associated reptiles and plants. In this excavation, the paleontologists are working downwards, bed by bed, and recording every fossil fragment. This allows a detailed reconstruction of life some 58 million years ago, when mammals were beginning to diversify.

they were a key part of the animal life, and of course in Australasia, until more recently. But, yet again, there is no clear evidence that marsupials are consistently worse at everything than the placentals.

What happens if we compare the mammals as a group, to other major animal groups, such as the reptiles? The dinosaurs and pterosaurs died out at the K-T event, and hence we might suggest that they were poorly adapted compared to the Late Cretaceous mammals. However, among the reptiles, the lizards, snakes, turtles and crocodilians survived. Hence, reptiles in general were just as good as the mammals at surviving.

The conclusion to these various discussions seems to be: it would be hard to support the contention that placental mammals survived the K-T event because they were better adapted than other groups. Was it simply luck, at a time when the normal principles of Darwinian evolution were in chaos?

Recovering from calamity

We now turn to the success of the placentals during the recovery phase. One might ask: why did frogs or turtles not diversify spectacularly, instead of mammals, and take over the broad range of ecological roles and lifestyles in the Palaeocene and Early Eocene? Certainly all of these groups had appeared at about the same time, in the Late Triassic (see pages 14-15), and they had all occupied specialized or "marginal" roles during the Age of Dinosaurs. The extinction of the dinosaurs cleared the way, so could any of them have taken over? This is where the mammals may have demonstrated their "superiority" – probably not in one of the more obvious characteristics noted above, such as speed or breeding abilities, but simply in their overall adaptability or versatility.

Versatility is a generalized feature of a group of plants or animals. It refers to its potential, in terms of the genes in the population, to diversify and occupy a broad range of biological roles. Turtles and frogs probably have low versatility, since they are both highly modified to rather specialized modes of life. The Late Cretaceous mammals, most of them being small, shrew-like insectivores, were generalists that could adapt more readily.

A contemporary representation of this idea is in discussions of which animals might survive a global nuclear war, and rule the Earth afterwards. The balance of argument often favours creatures such as rats or locusts, rather than gorillas or elephants. The first two groups are able to breed fast and to eat almost anything, unlike the last two.

The rest of this chapter considers the radiation of the placentals during this early phase of the Age of Mammals. The evolution of marsupials and other groups, in South America and Australia, will be discussed in chapter four.

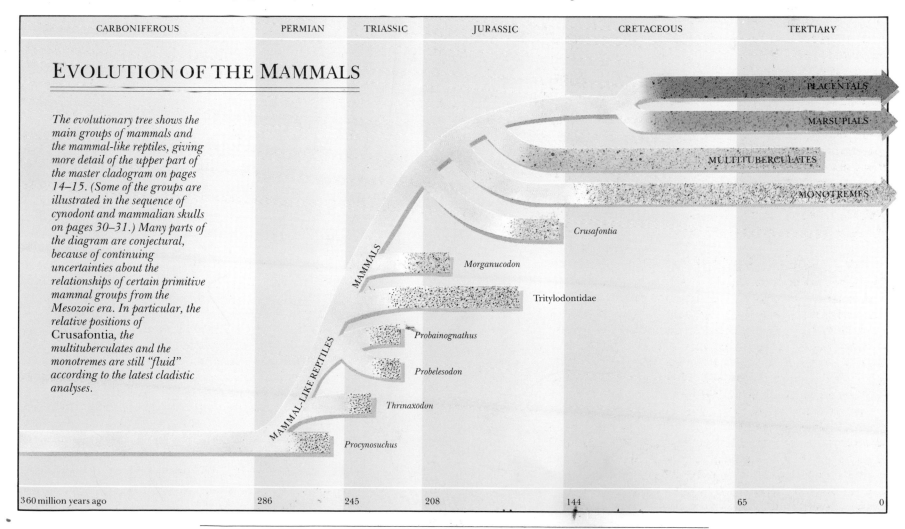

EVOLUTION OF THE MAMMALS

The evolutionary tree shows the main groups of mammals and the mammal-like reptiles, giving more detail of the upper part of the master cladogram on pages 14–15. (Some of the groups are illustrated in the sequence of cynodont and mammalian skulls on pages 30–31.) Many parts of the diagram are conjectural, because of continuing uncertainties about the relationships of certain primitive mammal groups from the Mesozoic era. In particular, the relative positions of **Crusafontia**, the multituberculates and the monotremes are still "fluid" according to the latest cladistic analyses.

CARBONIFEROUS · PERMIAN · TRIASSIC · JURASSIC · CRETACEOUS · TERTIARY

PLACENTALS
MARSUPIALS
MULTITUBERCULATES
MONOTREMES

MAMMALS

Crusafontia
Morganucodon
Tritylodontidae
Probainognathus
Probelesodon
Thrinaxodon

MAMMAL-LIKE REPTILES

Procynosuchus

360 million years ago · 286 · 245 · 208 · 144 · 65 · 0

Crazy Mountain mammals

The best way to appreciate the scale of the early adaptive radiation among placental mammals is to look at a single fossil-rich site in detail, and to compare it with the situation in the Late Cretaceous, before the great extinction. A suitable example, because it has been extensively studied, is the Fort Union Formation of the Crazy Mountain Basin, Montana, USA, which is dated as Late Palaeocene (63–58 million years ago).

Five or six million years before, Montana was dominated by dinosaurs. This US state has yielded several well-known types of dinosaur from almost the end of the Cretaceous period. The fossils show that the broad lowland plains beside the mid-American sea – a strip of salt water that once divided North America into two – were full of tropical vegetation, that was grazed by horned dinosaurs like *Triceratops* and crested hadrosaurs such as *Parasaurolophus* and *Maiasaura*. These large herbivores were preyed on by *Tyrannosaurus*, the largest meat-eater, and one of the best-known dinosaurs with its massive jaws, powerful hindlimbs and tiny arms each equipped with only two short fingers. Smaller animals included lizards, snakes, turtles and birds.

Fossil mammal bones dating to just after the extinction of the dinosaurs were first collected in the Fort Union Formation by Earl Douglass, in 1901. Large collections of bones from small and medium-sized mammals were made

An artist's reconstruction of the head of Plesiadapis cooki *(above), based on specimens from the Upper Polecat Bench Formation of Little Sand Coulee, Wyoming. This Palaeocene tree-dweller was often classified as a primate (a member of the monkey and ape group), but recent analysis suggests that this is not the case.*

The skeleton of the small apatemyid Heterohyus nanus *(opposite) from the Messel pit, near Frankfurt, Germany. The two spindly fingers on each hand have only recently been recognized: they were probably used for extracting insects from deep within rotting wood.*

at a number of localities over the next few years, and by 1937, George Gaylord Simpson, one of the leading paleontologists of this century, was able to publish a detailed account of Fort Union animal life.

Simpson described 79 species of mammals from different localities. A typical example from the Gidley and Silberling Quarries is dominated by multituberculates (see page 37) such as *Ptilodus*, a tree-dwelling herbivore. Other mammals belonged to familiar modern groups, such as the lemur-like primate *Plesiadapis* – an early representative of the group to which apes, monkeys and humans belong – as well as shrew-like insectivores and cat-like carnivores. Most of the mammals, however, belonged to groups that are less familiar to us – for example, the entirely extinct insect-eating leptictids, pig-like taeniodonts and sheep-sized pantodonts (see page 48).

The Late Palaeocene world, 58 million years ago, was warmer and more humid than it is now. The Fort Union fossil plants include ferns, horsetails, grasses and sedges, a fan-palm, conifers, poplars, sycamores, oak, alder, chestnut, hazel, maple, elm, magnolia, hickory, walnut, birch, beech and fig! Associated fossil animals include snails, fishes, turtles, crocodilians and lizards, all of which point to a damp, warm habitat.

The Gidley Quarry fossil specimens are single bones, often fractured but not worn, and the rocks they are preserved in suggest the bed of a stream. The variety of species present suggests that the mammals fell into the water, or were dragged in by crocodilians, and the bones were pulled apart and broken by predators.

The Fort Union remains are typical of the Palaeocene in containing no mammals larger than modern sheep. Further, although some of the mammal groups represented are still with us today, some three-quarters of the species belong to extinct families. These less familiar forms will be looked at first.

Dining on insects and shellfish

Some of the most common small Palaeocene mammals were the multituberculates (see page 37), the longest-lived mammalian order. They were by no means a "holdover" group in the Palaeocene, surviving only by the "skin of their teeth" in a world of progressively advanced placentals. Multituberculates made up 10–15 per cent of all mammals within typical Palaeocene fossil collections in North America and Europe, and there was no indication that they were much lower on the cladogram than the placentals and marsupials.

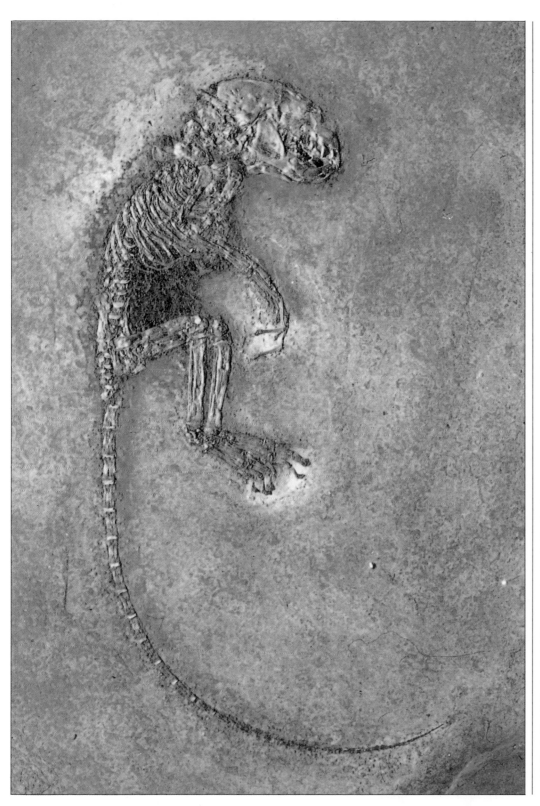

Another group to have survived from the Cretaceous were the leptictids – small, insect-eating placental mammals from the Late Cretaceous to the Oligocene in Asia and North America. *Leptictis*, a typical late form, had a long, shrew-like snout lined with small sharp teeth, that would have been ideal for puncturing the tough body casings of insects. The leptictids may be related to early placentals such as *Zalambdalestes*, or to the true insectivores such as shrews and hedgehogs.

The pantolestids, which lived from the Palaeocene to the Oligocene, were otter-like animals with broad, thickly-enamelled molar teeth, which they may have used for crushing shellfish. Their tail and bodily proportions, as seen in *Buxolestes* from the Eocene Messel rocks of Germany (see page 55), were very like those of an otter, so they may have been partly aquatic.

The apatemyids, also known from the Palaeocene to Oligocene, were another small group of insect-eaters with no obvious close relatives. *Sinclairella*, a North American apatemyid, epitomized the strange dentition of this group, which was a mix of insectivore and rodent types. The cheek teeth were adapted for puncturing insect skins, while the front incisors were extremely long and rat-like. A recently discovered skeleton shows that the apatemyids had two very long fingers on each hand, which may have been used for winkling out insects from tree bark. The relationships of the apatemyids are a mystery: were they aberrant insectivores or carnivores?

The anagalids, a group that survived from the Late Cretaceous to the Oligocene, dominated Palaeocene fossil assemblages in Asia. *Anagale* itself had generalized teeth set in a rather weak lower jaw: the broad cheek teeth suggest a diet of plants. The anagalids are often re-constructed as being rather rabbit-like in appearance and habits, and indeed the two groups may be related.

Rooters and browsers

Some of the smaller Palaeocene mammals were herbivores, but probably in specialized ways. There were also several important groups of larger animals that fed on plants, either by digging up underground roots, stems and tubers – the rooters – or by feeding on leaves, buds and fruits from low bushes – the browsers. True grasses were only just coming on the scene, and there were as yet no large grasslands in Palaeocene or Eocene times for grazing animals. Such landscapes developed later, in the Oligocene and Miocene (see chapters three to (Continued on page 48.)

DIVERSIFICATION OF THE MAMMALS

The mammals had existed for nearly as long as the dinosaurs, some 150 million years, before they began to diversify and become more common during the Palaeocene and early Eocene epochs. The most dramatic part of this classic "adaptive radiation" lasted from 65 to 55 million years ago. During this time the placental mammals diversified, from the three or four families that survived the end-of-Cretaceous mass extinction, to well over forty. All the living orders of placentals, from bats and whales to primates and horses, came on the scene during these crucial years.

The evolutionary tree (far right) shows the rapid branching of mammalian lineages that took place during the Palaeocene and Early Eocene. Some branching was under way during the Late Cretaceous, when the dinosaurs were still around. The pattern of evolution was rapid, and focused just before and shortly after the beginning of the Palaeocene. The skeletons and skulls show the diversity of these "experimental" lineages during the Palaeocene. These groups gave way to more "modern" forms of placental mammals during the Eocene epoch.

Typically, Palaeocene mammals were smaller than later forms. Uintatherium (1) was the size of a small rhinoceros, while Titanoides (2) and Mesonyx (3) were equivalent to large sheep.

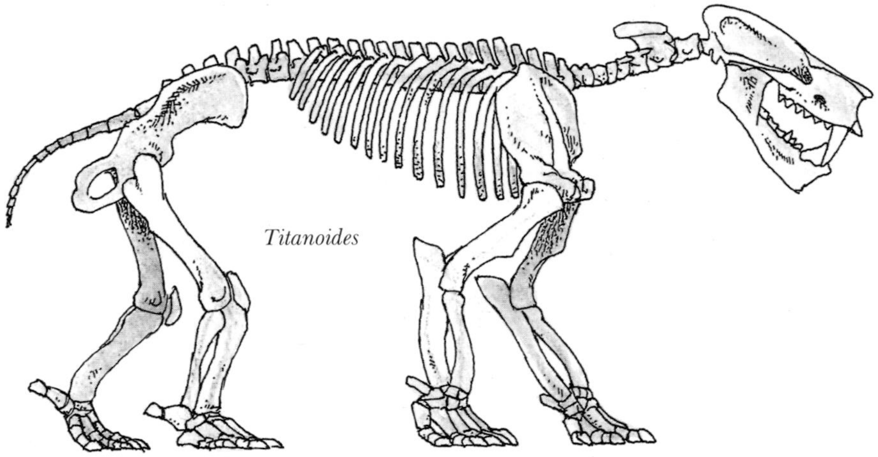

Titanoides

Titanoides (above), a pantodont, was a terrestrial herbivore that may have looked rather bear-like in life. The large canine teeth may have been used for grubbing up food, or for fighting. The skull of the apatemyid Sinclairella (right) was small, about 60 millimetres (2 inches) long, and looks even more like that of a carnivore. However, the huge incisor teeth were seemingly for cracking hard insects.

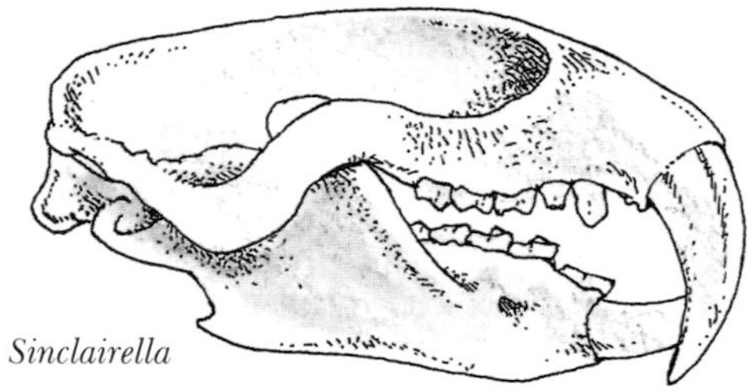

Sinclairella

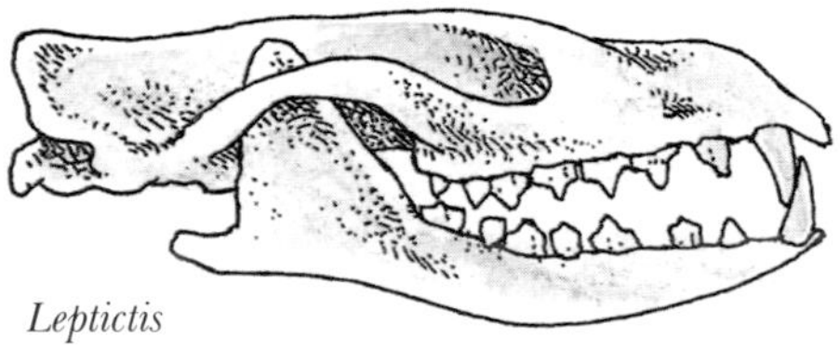

The skull of an insectivore, Leptictis (left), showing the array of small, sharp teeth. The mesonychid Mesonyx (below) was a carnivore some 1.5 metres (5 feet) long, that may have fed on the other creatures shown on these pages.

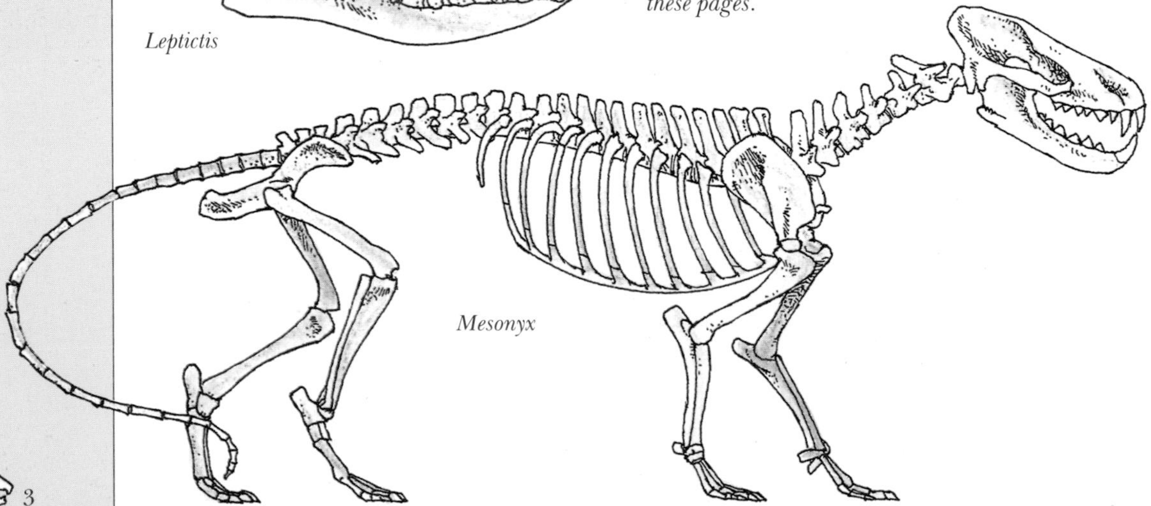

Leptictis

Mesonyx

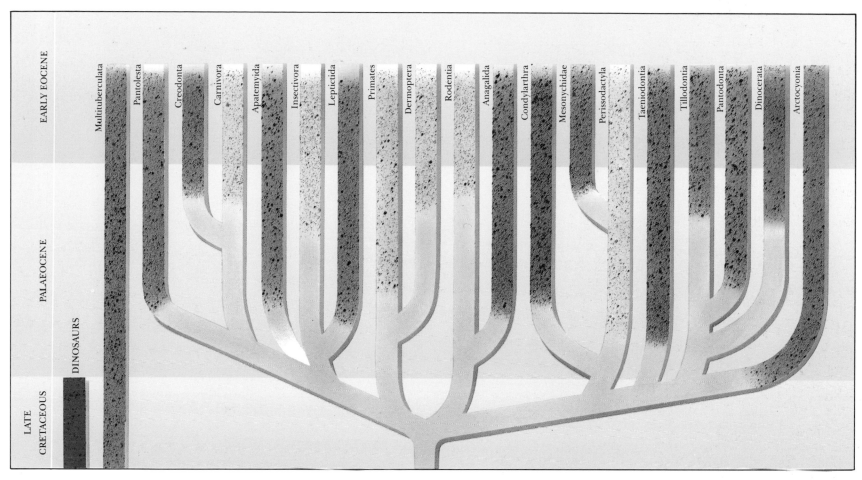

EARLY EOCENE

PALAEOCENE

LATE CRETACEOUS

DINOSAURS

Multituberculata
Pantolesta
Creodonta
Carnivora
Apatemyida
Insectivora
Leptictida
Primates
Dermoptera
Rodentia
Anagalida
Condylarthra
Mesonychidae
Perissodactyla
Taeniodontia
Tillodontia
Pantodonta
Dinocerata
Arctocyonia

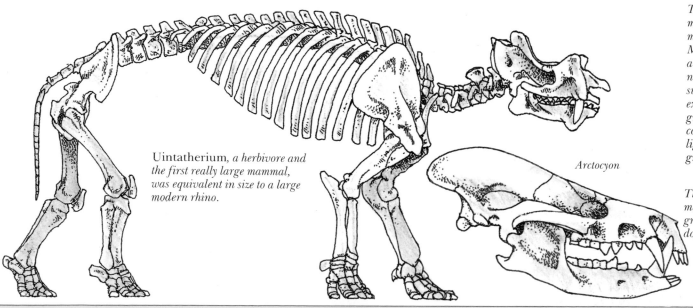

Uintatherium, *a herbivore and the first really large mammal, was equivalent in size to a large modern rhino.*

Arctocyon

The radiation of the placental mammals during the first 10 million years of the Age of Mammals, in North America and Europe (above). About 18 new groups arose, of which six survive today. This diagram excludes extinct and modern groups from the southern continents. The lineages in the lighter shading indicate the groups are still living.

The skull of Arctocyon (left), a member of an early herbivorous group – despite its superficially dog-like design.

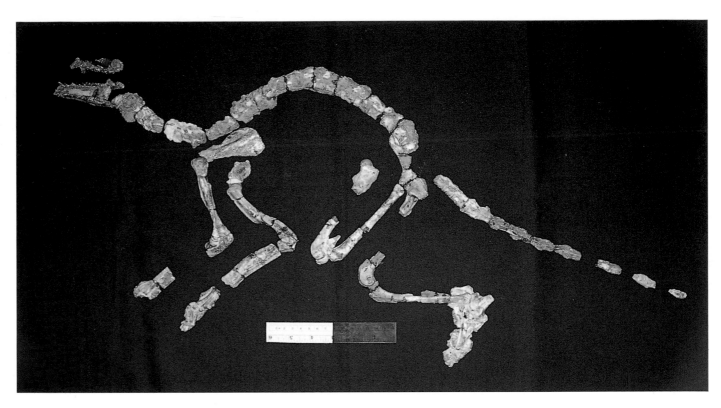

A skeleton of Chriacus, *an arctocyonid "condylarth", from Early Eocene rocks of the Bighorn Basin, Wyoming, USA. The damaged skull (top left) shows teeth with herbivorous adaptations, and the long limbs and flexible spine suggest that this animal could run quite fast.*

five), and led to new types of mammal.

The taeniodonts, such as *Stylinodon*, were bulky North American mammals that ranged up to pig-sized. The short limbs were rather unusual in that the fore limb was larger than the hind limb, and the claws were very like those of a digging animal. The lower jaw was deep, the cheek teeth broad and high-crowned, and the canines and incisors long – especially the canines. In addition the teeth bore enamel, the hard outer covering of the tooth, only on one side, and the crowns of the teeth were worn nearly smooth, but with a sharp cutting edge formed by the worn enamel. Such teeth suggest a diet of tough plant parts such as roots and tubers, and the digging claws were probably used to grub up food.

The tillodonts were another small group of rooting mammals. They are known mainly from their skulls, which look rather taeniodont-like at first. However, the largest teeth are the incisors, not the canines, and there is a clear gap between the front teeth and the cheek teeth. This is called the diastema and is a common feature of herbivores. Tillodonts were up to bear-sized, and their diet was probably similar to that of the taeniodonts. Their relationships to other mammals are a mystery.

The pantodonts, a third group of Palaeocene herbivores, may be related to the tillodonts. They include 25 genera from North America, Europe and Asia, some as large as a hippopotamus, and some feeding by rooting while others browsed. One of the larger types was *Titanoides* which had massive limbs, plantigrade feet – that is, soles flat on the ground as in humans and bears – and digging claws on its hands. The dentition was primitive, with all teeth of much the same shape and no diastema, but male *Titanoides* had long canine teeth, which may have been used in contests for mates.

The arctocyonids were smaller animals, and they included Late Cretaceous forms such as *Protungulatum*, the first placental true herbivore. The Palaeocene *Arctocyon*, whose fossils are known from Europe and North America, was a sheep-sized animal that probably looked more like a dog. Its broad molars were adapted for crushing plant food rather than for tearing flesh. But its sharp incisors and canines, on the other hand, suggest that *Arctocyon* may have taken a mixed omnivorous diet.

The coming of the "condylarths"

The relationships of the arctocyonids are uncertain, but they are usually associated with a very large mammal group, the "condylarths". This group contains over 100 genera which are usually put together but may not be closely linked. The group may contain as many as five or six separate evolutionary lineages, whose origins may have been close to those of the modern ungulate groups such as horses, cows, pigs and elephants (see chapter three).

Early "condylarths", such as *Ectoconus*, were like *Arctocyon* in many respects. They had a generalized dentition and a primitive skeleton which was little modified from that of early placentals (see page 38). Some, such as *Hyopsodus*, were much smaller – about the size of a hedgehog – and rather like an insectivore in appearance, although the teeth suggest herbivory.

Phenacodus, representing another "condylarth" lineage, is often placed close to the ancestry of horses. It was about the size of a sheep, with long and primitive limb bones. Supposedly horse-like characters were that the two outer toes had become shortened, leaving the middle three meeting the ground, as in certain early horses; also, the cheek teeth had broad, grinding surfaces.

The largest mammals in the Late Palaeocene and Eocene epochs were the dinocerates, or uintatheres, of North America and Asia. They are better known from the

UINTATHERIUM

The dinocerates were the first large mammals. They looked broadly like rhinos or hippos, but were entirely unrelated. The set of six blunt-headed "horns" on the head were presumably used in sexual displays, when males tried to impress females; the large canine teeth may also have been used in fights of this sort. The body of this creature was 3.5 metres (11 feet) long, yet its brain was only about the size of a clenched human fist.

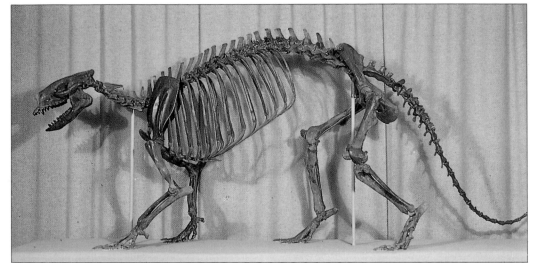

A skeleton of the herbivorous "condylarth" Phenacodus, from the Early Eocene deposits of the Bighorn Basin, Wyoming, USA. This creature is often said to be close to the ancestry of horses. The skeleton shows primitive features such as short limbs, five fingers and toes, and a small braincase.

The skull of the mesonychid Mesonyx *from the Middle Eocene rocks of Twin Buttes, Wyoming, USA (below). This animal was the same size as* Phenacodus *(right), and the skeleton was broadly similar, but the teeth show clearly that it was a carnivore: the cheek teeth were triangular and pointed for tearing flesh, rather than flattened for crushing plant material.*

Eocene, when creatures such as *Uintatherium* roamed the forests and plains of Utah, USA. This massive beast was as large as a rhinoceros, and had bony protuberances on its head that were characteristic of the group. Broad cheek teeth clearly indicate herbivory. Male specimens had canine teeth 15 centimetres (6 inches) long that, as in today's hippopotamus, may have been used in fighting; contests were a possible function of the bony knobs on the cranium, too.

The brains of uintatheres were remarkably small. In fact, this is not an uncommon feature of the "first wave" of placental mammals. The relationships of the uintatheres are as mysterious as those of most other herbivorous groups just described. They have at various times been allied with the artocyonids, the anagalids, and even some of the South American ungulates.

Giant skulls for land or sea

The largest carnivorous mammals in the Palaeocene were, oddly enough, ungulates – a group which is today wholly herbivorous, including horses, cattle and elephants. The mesonychids, such as *Mesonyx*, were about wolf-sized and broadly similar to *Arctocyon* in appearance. However, fossils reveal that the molar teeth were pointed and adapted for cutting flesh, like those of a dog or cat, yet broad enough for crushing bones. *Mesonyx* was adapted for fast running but, oddly for a carnivore, it had the characteristic ungulate hooves instead of claws on its feet.

Some of the later mesonychids became giants. *Andrewsarchus*, from the Late Eocene of Mongolia, had a vast skull, 83 centimetres (33 inches) long and 56 centimetres (22 inches) wide, larger than any other terrestrial carnivorous mammal. In life, its body length is estimated to have been 5–6 metres (16–19 feet) or more. The mesonychids are often described as one of the "condylarth" lineages, and they show affinities with the arctocyonids and the whales. Indeed, the skulls of early whales were almost indistinguishable from that of *Mesonyx* (see page 46).

The other main carnivore group of this time was the creodonts, 50 genera that were the main meat-eaters in North America, Europe and Asia during the Late Palaeocene and Eocene epochs. Creodonts ranged from stoat- to bear-sized, and show major advances towards the modern carnivorous mammals. *Sinopa*, an early fox-like creodont, had a low skull, and all of its cheek teeth were sharpened for slicing flesh. In fact on each side of the jaw, the upper molars 1 and/or 2, and the lower molars 2 or 3, were modified to form narrow longitudinal blades. These are called carnassial or flesh-shearing teeth, as seen in today's carnivores, although modern carnassials are the upper premolar 4 and lower molar 1. *Oxyaena*, a creodont that resembled a cat, had a long body and short limbs, while the contemporary *Hyaenodon* had longer limbs and a digitgrade posture, up on its toes, unlike the flat-footed

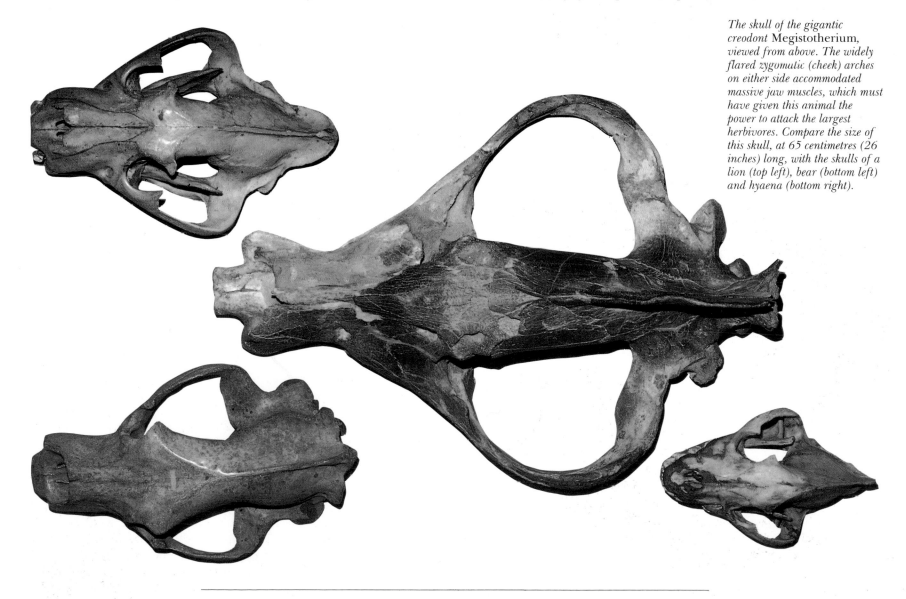

The skull of the gigantic creodont Megistotherium, *viewed from above. The widely flared zygomatic (cheek) arches on either side accommodated massive jaw muscles, which must have given this animal the power to attack the largest herbivores. Compare the size of this skull, at 65 centimetres (26 inches) long, with the skulls of a lion (top left), bear (bottom left) and hyaena (bottom right).*

plantigrade, *Oxyaena*. Some later hyaenodonts reached a huge size, with skulls up to 65 centimetres (26 inches) long. The creodonts are generally regarded as partly ancestral to the modern carnivores, the cats, dogs, weasels, bears and seals.

These two groups of early carnivorous mammals, mesonychids and creodonts, covered the spectrum of sizes very well, and included a number of giants that must have been able to prey on the larger herbivores such as the dinocerates. All of these groups gave way in piecemeal fashion, during the Eocene and Oligocene, to the more modern groups of herbivores and carnivores.

The great mammalian radiation

The rapid evolution of placental mammals in North America, Europe and Asia during some 10 million years of the Palaeocene and Early Eocene, ranks as the best-known example of what is called adaptive radiation (see page 40). During this time, the 15 or so lineages of now extinct mammals described above diversified widely in most parts of the world. In addition, several of the living mammalian orders arose during this time: the insectivores, "modern" carnivores, dermopterans or "flying lemurs", bats, primates, perissodactyls or horses and rhinos, pholidotans or pangolins, and rodents. (The insectivores and pri-

A skull of the creodont Hyaenodon *from the Eocene–Oligocene Phosphorites deposits of Caylus, France. The skull was relatively large in proportion to the body, but otherwise there are few obvious differences from modern carnivores.*

mates, and possibly others, may have come on the scene a little earlier, at the very end of the Late Cretaceous.) The other modern mammalian orders – the lagomorphs or rabbits, artiodactyls or cows, pigs and deer, proboscideans or elephants, cetaceans or whales, and sirenians or sea cows – all appeared during the subsequent 22 million years of the Eocene.

The great mammalian radiation represented a major increase in the global diversity of families, from 15 in the latest Cretaceous, to 32 in the Early Palaeocene, 68 in the Late Palaeocene, and 78 in the Early Eocene. The early increase is even more dramatic than these figures suggest, since 5 of the 15 mammal families from the end of the Cretaceous disappeared at the K-T boundary (see page 40). Hence, the rise in the Palaeocene and Early Eocene was from only 10 "holdover" families to 32, 68 and 78 – rises of 220, 112 and 15 per cent respectively. The rate of diversification, then, was extremely rapid at first, and slowed down markedly after the end of the Palaeocene.

At the level of genera, which are smaller groupings within families, the increase is just as striking: 40 or so genera worldwide in the Late Cretaceous and about the same number (although different ones) in the Early Palaeocene, to about 120 in the Late Palaeocene, and 200 in the Early Eocene.

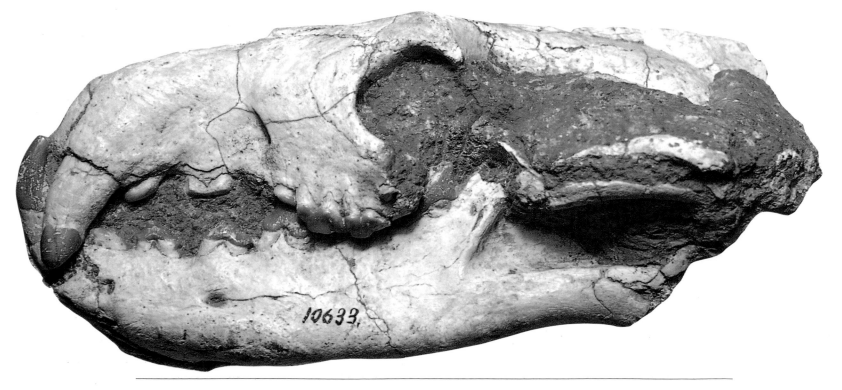

SPECIALIZATIONS OF MAMMALS

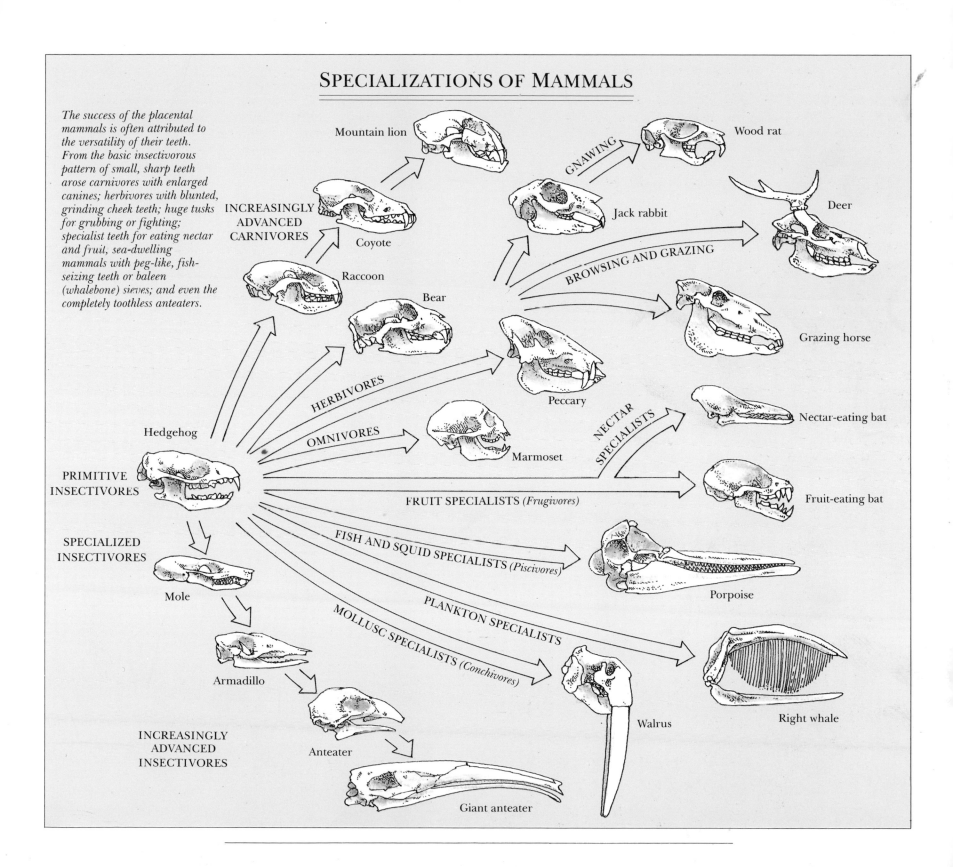

The success of the placental mammals is often attributed to the versatility of their teeth. From the basic insectivorous pattern of small, sharp teeth arose carnivores with enlarged canines; herbivores with blunted, grinding cheek teeth; huge tusks for grubbing or fighting; specialist teeth for eating nectar and fruit, sea-dwelling mammals with peg-like, fish-seizing teeth or baleen (whalebone) sieves; and even the completely toothless anteaters.

INCREASINGLY ADVANCED CARNIVORES

Mountain lion

Coyote

Raccoon

Bear

GNAWING

Wood rat

Jack rabbit

Deer

BROWSING AND GRAZING

Grazing horse

Peccary

HERBIVORES

OMNIVORES

Marmoset

NECTAR SPECIALISTS

Nectar-eating bat

FRUIT SPECIALISTS (*Frugivores*)

Fruit-eating bat

Hedgehog

PRIMITIVE INSECTIVORES

SPECIALIZED INSECTIVORES

Mole

FISH AND SQUID SPECIALISTS (*Piscivores*)

Porpoise

PLANKTON SPECIALISTS

MOLLUSC SPECIALISTS (*Conchivores*)

Armadillo

Anteater

Walrus

Right whale

INCREASINGLY ADVANCED INSECTIVORES

Giant anteater

The change was thus dramatic at the global level. It was also dramatic when individual fossil sites are considered. Typical well-preserved collections of animal fossils from the Late Cretaceous of North America contain 20–30 mammalian species, while Middle Palaeocene faunas have twice as many. Hence, the diversity of mammals at any locality had doubled.

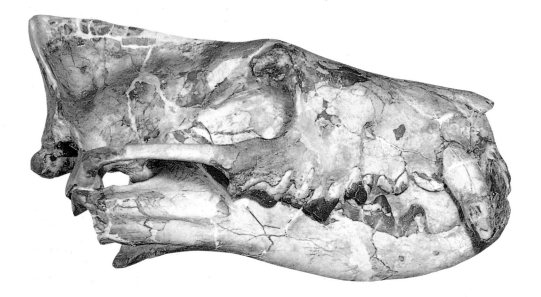

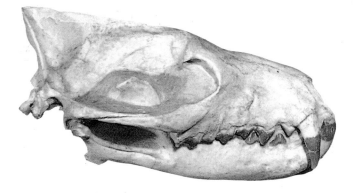

The fossil skulls of Hyaenodon horridus *(top) and* H. crucians *(middle and bottom), all from the Middle Oligocene of South Dakota, USA. Many species of* Hyaenodon *are known, some as small as stoats, and others larger than hyaenas. The skulls vary not only in size but also in shape; the largest shown here is relatively higher and more "snub-nosed" than the others. Such a change in shape with increasing size can also be seen in the two smaller specimens, even though they are the same species. Members of the* Hyaenodon *genus are known from Europe, North America, Asia and Africa. They were highly successful carnivores.*

This could be explained simply by the removal of the dinosaurs, which emptied "ecospace" that was soon filled by mammals. However, few of the Palaeocene mammals could fill all of the dinosaur lifestyles, especially those of the giant forms.

Some of the increase in mammalian diversity during the Palaeocene must be explained by their greater specialization. The ecological roles, or "niches", occupied by Palaeocene mammals may well have been more restricted in size than those of typical Cretaceous representatives. This process has, in part, permitted mammals to become more and more specialized, and so more diverse, than the dinosaurs.

Evolution in theory and practice

The post-dinosaur phase of mammalian history illustrates well the theoretical model of an adaptive radiation, which can be divided into four stages.

First, an initial short phase of rapid evolution in which many kinds of "experimental" lineages may be spawned; radiation is essentially unconstrained by competition with other animals or similar normal ecological processes, because of the large amount of empty "ecospace" following a major extinction.

Second, a longer phase of stabilization, lasting for most of the Palaeocene and Early Eocene in this case, in which the "experimental" lineages sort themselves out and settle down into particular niches; normal ecological interactions resume as the "ecospace" fills up.

Third, high levels of extinction of many of the early "experimental" lineages that may not be so well adapted as others; in our case, many of the lines of mammalian herbivores and carnivores already described did not outlive the Early Eocene.

Fourth, an extended period of low turnover, in which the successful lineages evolve slowly, and very few new lineages arise or older ones become extinct.

After the initial 10 million years of the Palaeocene and earliest Eocene, most of the first three stages had passed, although the whole sorting-out operation may have lasted until the end of the Eocene, a total span of 30 million years. (This span is diminishing all of the time, as fresh fossil discoveries of ever-older representatives of the modern mammalian orders are found.) Nevertheless, the Middle Eocene was still a time of flux for the mammals, with representatives of many of the Palaeocene groups still holding out against a whole range of ancestors of the more familiar modern orders.

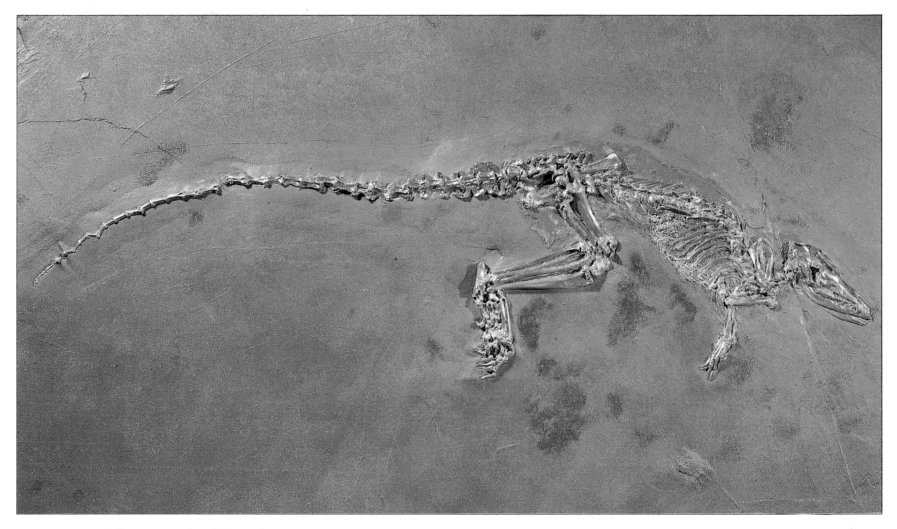

The mammals of Messel

Certain fossil deposits have become celebrated because they display exceptional preservation: soft-bodied animals such as worms or jellyfish may be present, as well as the soft parts of skeletonized animals, including guts, skin and muscles. These exceptional localities, or Lagerstatten as they are called, have often been regarded as curiosities, fun to look at because of the remarkable quality of the fossils, but otherwise of little use. However, now that a relatively large number of such Lagerstatten are known, they are regarded as examples of what life was really like. The more usual fossil deposits of a few scattered bones or shells are now seen as deficient, but good enough for filling the gaps in our knowledge between the Lagerstatten.

The best-preserved fossils of mammals for this early

A spectacular and complete skeleton of the small, active, bipedal Leptictidium nasutum *from the Messel pit, near Frankfurt. Every part is preserved in place, right down to the smallest toe bone and the last vertebra of the tail. Even the body outline is preserved, with traces of hair, internal organs and gut contents.*

period have been found in the Middle Eocene (50 million years old) oil shales at Messel, near Frankfurt, Germany. A giant pit was excavated at Messel from 1886 to 1971 for the extraction of oil shale, which was distilled to produce one million tonnes of crude oil. Fossil vertebrates were first found there in 1875, but vast new collections have been made since commercial operations ended. Details of the hair, stomach contents and even internal organs of the animals have been preserved.

The fossil skeletons proved very hard to extract since oil shales contain up to 40 per cent water; on drying, the particles fall apart and the fossils can be lost. So a new preparation technique was developed to cope with this. The broken surface of the oil shale lump is covered with synthetic resin, which stabilizes the fossil. The sediment

(Continued on page 58.)

THE MIDDLE EOCENE MAMMALS OF MESSEL

The plants and animals in this scene can be reconstructed more accurately than for almost any other time, because of the remarkable quality of preservation in the 50-million-year-old Messel deposits. The climate was warm and humid, and over the years, many layers of decaying plant material fell into the lake, gradually accumulating to form a thick deposit of oil shale. Plant leaves, animal skeletons and sometimes whole organisms were preserved. The fossilized mammals include a mixture of ancient forms, such as creodonts and leptictids, as well as early representatives of more modern groups such as primates, rhinos, horses, anteaters and pangolins.

The world as it was then.

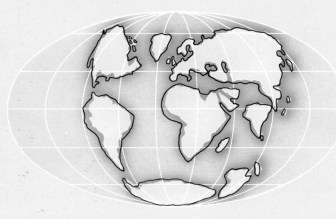

The majority of mammals in the Messel deposits are small. They include the primate Necrolemur *(1), the lepticid* Leptictidium *(2), and the early cat-like carnivore* Miacis *(3).* Eurotamandua *(4) is an anteater. Also shown are the pangolin* Eomanis *(5), the* creodont Hyaenodon *(6),* Propalaeotherium *(7) a type of "horse" and* Lophiodon *(8), an early tapir.*

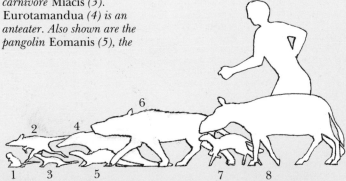

particles are then removed from the outside, giving a perfect intact fossil embedded in a resin "matrix".

The Messel deposits also contain abundant plant remains which suggest a range of forest trees such as laurel, oak, beech, citrus fruits, vines and palms, with a few conifers, and ponds covered with lilies. These plants indicate a humid tropical or subtropical climate. Invertebrate fossils found in the deposits include snails and insects, while fishes account for nine-tenths of the vertebrate fossils. Amphibians and reptiles are generally rare, although some frogs, salamanders, crocodilians, tortoises, lizards and snakes have been discovered. The birds include waders as well as the large flightless predator, *Diatryma*, which was superficially similar to contemporary giant meat-eating birds in South America.

The mammal fossils constitute only 2–3 per cent of the vertebrate finds, but they have attracted most attention. So far some 35 species, belonging to 13 orders, have been identified. They include the marsupial opossums, several primitive insect-eaters, the pantolestid *Buxolestes* (see page 45), and a few true insectivores (see page 62).

A prehistoric "leprechaun"

One remarkable recent find is the small leptictid (see page 45) *Leptictidium*. Its skeleton shows that it was a biped (two-legged walker), standing only 20 centimetres (8 inches) high, that dashed about like a long-tailed leprechaun.

The early ungulate Messelobunodon *(right), an animal close to the ancestry of pigs, cattle and camels. The deep jaws accommodated grinding teeth and the long limbs were a typical feature of more advanced herbivores.*

The skull and scattered neck vertebrae of the tapir Lophiodon *(below). Today, tapirs are known from South America and southern Asia, but formerly they were important in the animal communities of Europe and North America. Note the nipping incisor teeth at the front of the jaws, followed by a gap, and then a row of flattened, grinding cheek teeth.*

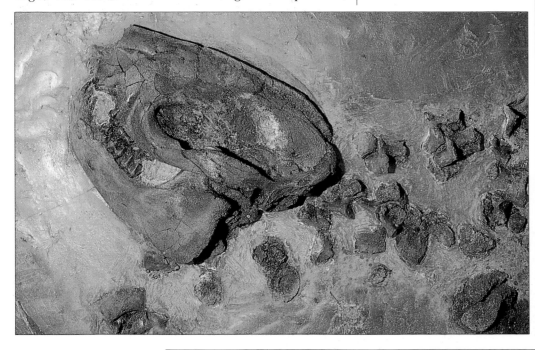

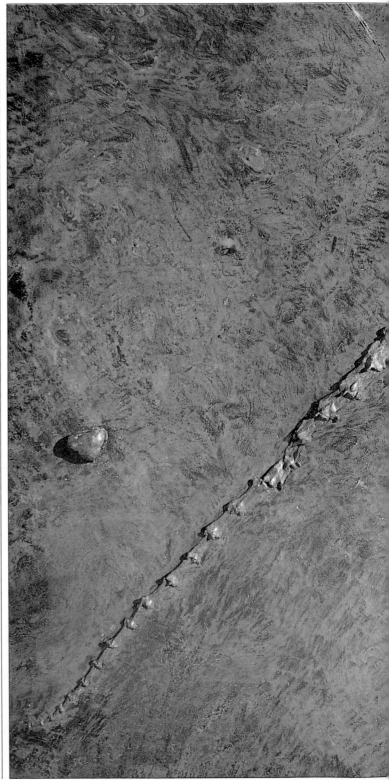

There is considerable evidence for this unusual posture. Three nearly complete skeletons show that its long tail made up about two-thirds of its entire length, that it had a short body , and relatively long hind limbs but short fore limbs. The long tail was probably used for maintaining balance, as in kangaroos and bipedal dinosaurs, and the short body and arms tend to confirm this. The body shape suggests that the creature's centre of gravity lay near the hip, as in humans, rather than somewhere between the fore and hind limbs, as in typical quadrupeds (four-legged walkers).

Leptictidium had small sharp teeth, and a detailed study of these and its jaws show that it was essentially a carnivore. In addition, the exceptional conditions of fossilization have allowed paleontologists to examine the last meal in three preserved carcasses of this little mammal.

In one specimen, several dozen pieces of bone were found, some of which could be ascribed confidently to a small lizard. The second carcass contained bones of an even smaller mammal, as yet unidentified, and the third included pieces of chitin from the casings of large insects. In all specimens, too, there were plant remains. So

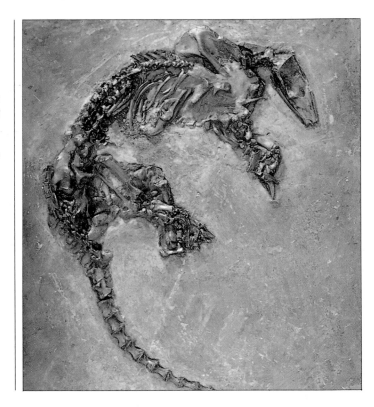

A fossilized skeleton of Eurotamandua *(right), a most surprising and recent find from the Messel deposits. This is the oldest known anteater, member of a group known otherwise only from South America (with a very recent spread into North America). The tubular, toothless snout would have housed a long, sticky tongue for extracting ants and termites from their nests.*

The early hedgehog Pholidocercus hassiacus *(below) from Messel, showing the primitive pattern of small, sharp, insectivorous teeth. The most striking feature is the preserved pelt of spiny fur over the creature's back.*

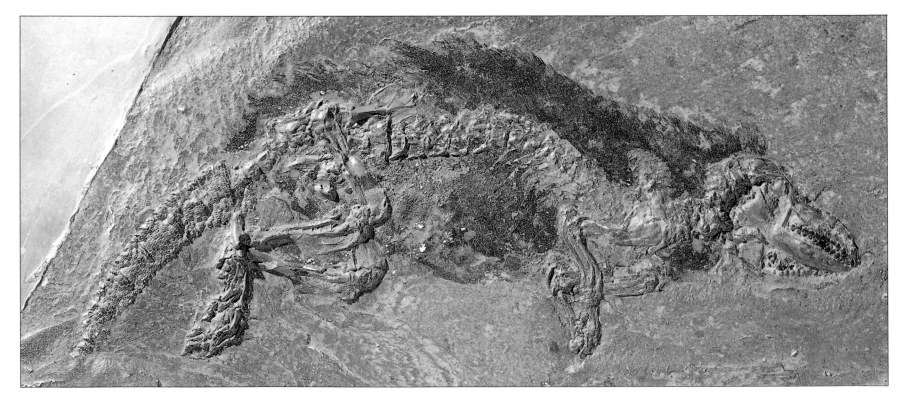

Lepticidium evidently had an omnivorous diet.

Other small mammals from Messel include six species of bats, the most abundant mammalian order represented. Some specimens have scales from butterfly wings and the cases of beetles preserved in their stomachs. There are also two species of lemur-like primates, and four squirrel-like rodents. The carnivores are a mixture of primitive and "modern" forms: a creodont and two species of miacids. The same is true of the herbivores: a "condylarth", three perissodactyls and three artiodactyls (see pages 48, 76 and 77).

Most of the Messel animals fit our expectations for an animal community from Europe or North America during the Eocene epoch, but two of the fossil mammals discovered there are a great mystery. One is the anteater *Eurotamandua*, a member of a group known otherwise only from South America. The other is the pangolin *Eomanis*, from a group typical of South-East Asia. How these animals came to be living in central Europe in the

A skeleton of the pangolin Eomanis, *which – like* Eurotamandua – *is an exotic element of the Messel community. Pangolins are otherwise known only from southern Asia. In life,* Eomanis *was covered with overlapping "scales" made from toughened mats of hair.*

Middle Eocene is a mystery, but they must have formerly been much more widespread than they are today.

Preserved a second time

The Messel quarry seems to represent an Eocene lake into which streams washed clay from the surrounding area. The lake filled periodically with organic matter, which led to algal "blooms" or overgrowths, and consequent deoxygenation of the water. Aquatic animals then died and fell to the bottom, while terrestrial animals were washed in, and birds and bats also fell into the lake. The oxygen-poor bottom waters prevented decay and scavenging, and the corpses were slowly covered and preserved as near-perfect fossils.

In 1981, the disused pit at Messel was designated as a dump for domestic and industrial waste. After an international campaign, the quarry was saved for science in 1989. The major research efforts on these spectacular fossils can now continue in the 1990s.

CHAPTER THREE

THE TURNING POINT

By Oligocene times (37–24 million years ago), most of the modern mammal groups had appeared. Indeed, the earliest ancestors of living groups date from the Late Cretaceous and Palaeocene, 30 million years before that, but most of them became fully established rather later. Several of the primitive groups already encountered in the Palaeocene and Eocene survived into the Oligocene, but they were declining and giving way to more familiar mammals such as hedgehogs, cats, dogs, beavers, horses, rhinos, elephants and whales.

The insect-chewers

The mammalian order Insectivora, which includes hedgehogs, moles and shrews, is often said to be "primitive" since the living forms are ecologically similar to many of the Mesozoic mammals from the Age of Dinosaurs. Certainly, the teeth of the earliest mammals are small and pointed, as in today's insect-eating shrews and hedgehogs, but there is no direct relationship. The earliest true Insectivora probably date from the Late Cretaceous, and certainly from the Palaeocene; the group may be related to the extinct leptictids of those times but it is no more ancient than many other living mammalian orders.

The oldest fossils of Insectivora are fragmentary shrew jaws from the Late Cretaceous. More complete fossils have been found only from the Late Palaeocene onwards. The shrews evolved during the Oligocene and Miocene to reach their present great diversity of 245 species.

The skull of the sabre-toothed cat Smilodon, one of the most striking of extinct mammals. This specimen dates from the Pleistocene epoch, but sabre-tooths have evolved several times since the Oligocene. The greatly enlarged canine teeth were an adaptation for piercing the thick hides of victims.

Moles, close relatives of shrews, arose in the Eocene. They are generally small animals which show exceptional adaptations for burrowing, particularly in the fore limbs, which are used for scooping soil backwards. The arm bones are broad and the hand is paddle-like, and often bears an additional sixth "finger". The mole's humerus, or upper arm bone, is a very characteristic broad bone with extra projections for the attachment of powerful shoulder muscles, for digging. This bone is readily recognized in collections of fossilized bones.

The third main insectivore group, the hedgehogs, also arose in the Eocene, although again, hedgehog-like insectivores date back to the Late Cretaceous. One of the most unusual hedgehogs was *Deinogalerix*, whose fossils come from Late Miocene rocks of southern Italy. It was five times the length of the living European hedgehog. *Deinogalerix* was not a spiny hedgehog but a hairy one, similar to the hairy hedgehogs found today in South-East Asia. The familiar spiny hedgehogs of Eurasia and Africa have sharp, stiff spines made from modified hairs, whereas the hairs are not so rigid in their hairy brethren. Nevertheless, *Deinogalerix* must have been a formidable animal!

The meat-eaters

The mammalian order Carnivora includes all major meat-eating mammals alive today: cats, dogs, hyaenas, weasels and seals. These animals are characterized by their diet of flesh, and in addition by their carnassial teeth, a feature also seen in the creodonts (see page 51).

PHYLOGENY OF THE "MODERN" MAMMALS

This cladogram summarises present knowledge of the relationships and distribution in time of all the living groups of mammals and their closest fossil relatives. The major mammalian subclasses – monotremes, marsupials and placentals – are shown in the general cladogram on page 43, which puts them in the context of other animal groups. The present phylogenetic tree represents the most detailed overview of all the major groups of mammals.

The monotremes and multituberculates branched off in the Late Jurassic, while the split between marsupials and placentals seems to have taken place in the Early Cretaceous: the oldest identifiable fossils that belong to one group or the other date from the beginning of the Late Cretaceous.

The remainder of the cladogram focuses on the placentals – the most familiar, and most diverse, subclass of mammals. All the living orders are shown (arrows to the right), ranging from proboscideans (elephants and relatives) to rodents (rats, hamsters, porcupines), and from cetaceans (whales, dolphins) to chiropterans (bats).

The exact relationships of many of these diverse mammalian orders are still very much disputed, despite extensive anatomical investigation and increasing study of their molecular similarities. Nevertheless, the fossils show that the placentals began to diversify *before* the end of the dinosaurs, in the Late Cretaceous, and about eight lineages must have survived that major extinction event to pass into the Palaeocene.

(Pli. = Pliocene; Ple. = Pleistocene)

million years ago   144

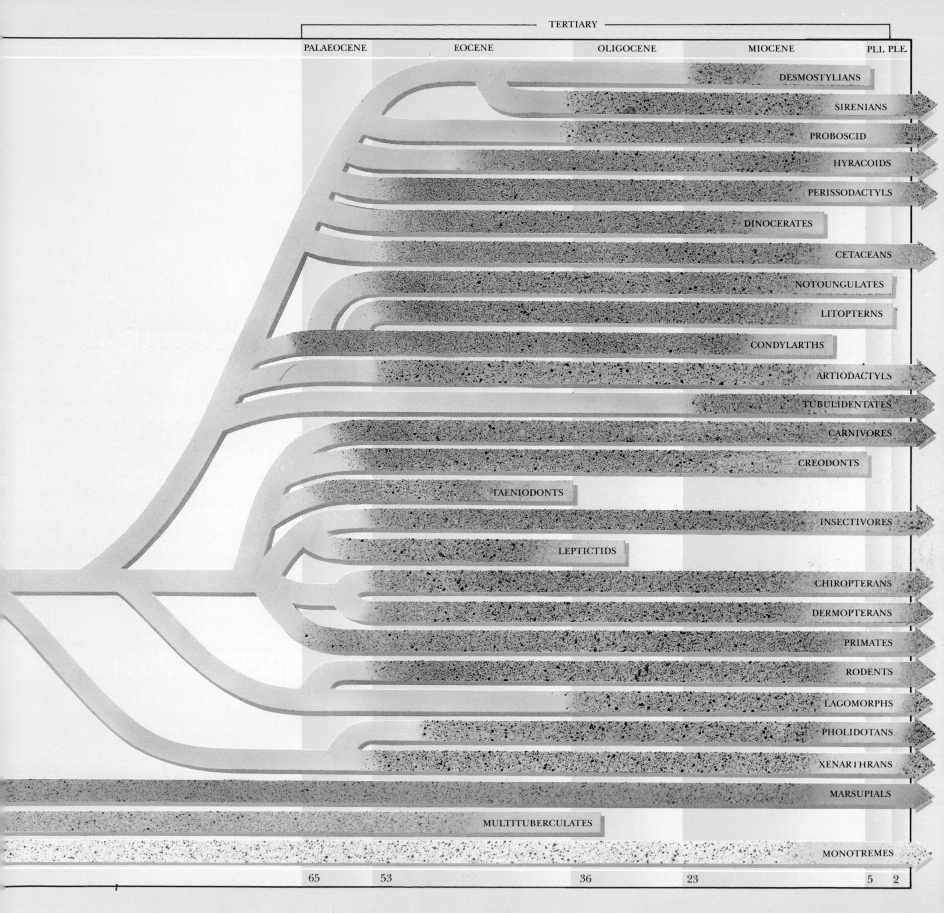

PALAEOCENE   EOCENE   OLIGOCENE   MIOCENE   PLI. PLE.

DESMOSTYLIANS

SIRENIANS

PROBOSCID

HYRACOIDS

PERISSODACTYLS

DINOCERATES

CETACEANS

NOTOUNGULATES

LITOPTERNS

CONDYLARTHS

ARTIODACTYLS

TUBULIDENTATES

CARNIVORES

CREODONTS

TAENIODONTS

INSECTIVORES

LEPTICTIDS

CHIROPTERANS

DERMOPTERANS

PRIMATES

RODENTS

LAGOMORPHS

PHOLIDOTANS

XENARTHRANS

MARSUPIALS

MULTITUBERCULATES

MONOTREMES

65   53   36   23   5   2

DEINOGALERIX

The giant fossil hedgehog Deinogalerix, from the Late Miocene beds of southern Italy, was as large as a terrier – five times longer than today's typical European hedgehog. Although modern species feed on insects and worms, Deinogalerix was probably an active hunter of smaller mammals, birds and reptiles. Unusually large animals are characteristic of isolated island communities. In Late Miocene times southern Italy consisted of several islands, and other animals of the time were similarly "island giants".

The carnassials of true carnivores are enlarged longitudinal blades, formed from the fourth premolar in the upper jaw and the first molar in the lower jaw (a different arrangement from creodonts). Their edges pass each other as the jaws close, and they cut flesh efficiently like a pair of shears. Over the course of carnivore evolution, the carnassial tooth blade has become larger, and it has moved from a diagonal orientation (at an angle to the jaw) to a longitudinal one (in line with the jaw), thus increasing its efficiency. Bone-crushing carnivores like the hyaenas also have broad, heavily-enamelled premolars which can withstand great wear. Of their other teeth, carnivores use their long canines for puncturing the skin of their prey, and their incisors for grasping and tearing flesh, as well as for grooming their fur.

The Carnivora may be related to the creodonts, but this is still uncertain. The oldest fossils of true carnivores date from the Late Palaeocene and Early Eocene, and many of these are miacids, such as *Miacis* from the Mid Eocene Messel remains in Germany (see page 55). Another early cat-like form was *Dinictis* of the Oligocene epoch, from South Dakota, USA; it had a lithe body, and powerful jaws. Its canine teeth were enlarged like daggers, for stabbing through the thick skin of larger herbivores.

The carnivores diverged into two main groups in the Late Eocene and Early Oligocene: the feliforms, comprising the cats, hyaenas and mongooses; and the caniforms, including dogs, bears, raccoons, weasels and seals. Most of the carnivore families just noted can be traced back to the Eocene and Oligocene.

note that when the elephants, rhinoceroses and other thick-skinned herbivores of Europe and North America died out in the Pleistocene, the sabre-toothed cats also disappeared.

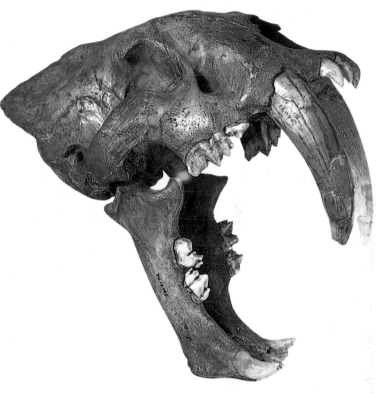

Daggers and sabres

The fossil record of cats is extensive, and it includes a much greater diversity of forms in the past than still survive today. In particular, most extinct cats have larger canine teeth than the present lions and tigers. So-called dagger teeth and sabre teeth appeared independently several times during the course of cat evolution, and such teeth in the placental mammal group are paralleled remarkably by the marsupial sabre-tooths of South America (see page 92). The sabre tooth is up to 15 centimetres (6 inches) long, with a backwards curve, and flattened from side to side; the lower jaw can be dropped very low to clear the tooth for stabbing at prey.

It was once thought that the sabre-toothed cats attacked large, thick-skinned prey by stabbing at their necks to sever the blood vessels or windpipe. However, the sabre teeth have rounded tips rather than sharp points, and the neck muscles needed for stabbing were probably not that strong. A new analysis of the jaws of the sabre-tooth *Smilodon* suggests that this cat used its sabres for cutting out chunks of flesh from its prey, rather than for stabbing. It is possible to imagine *Smilodon* attacking younger, vulnerable individuals by snapping superficially at the neck region, and levering out a piece of flesh weighing perhaps one or two kilograms (two to four pounds). The prey was then left to bleed to death. It is pertinent to

The Pleistocene sabre-toothed cat Smilodon's *skeleton (above) and skull (right). The sabre teeth were used to slice the flesh and blood vessels of the prey, causing them to bleed to death. When the jaws were shut, the sabres ran down on either side of the lower jaw, outside the mouth. These beautifully preserved specimens are typical of hundreds extracted from the Rancho La Brea tar pits in Los Angeles, California, USA. The pits were natural tar seeps that would have been covered with dry leaves and pools of water. Various animals walked across the surface in search of water, and became trapped. The sabre-tooths moved in for an easy meal – and became trapped as well.*

Bear-dogs and sealions

Dog-like carnivores evolved in Eocene and Oligocene times. The amphicyonids, such as *Daphoenus* from the Oligocene of North America, were large animals that had short limbs, flat feet and broad, bear-like skulls – hence their other name, the "bear dogs". Bears later became successful, particularly in the northern hemisphere. The extinct cave bear of Europe is known from abundant remains in the caves it used as a refuge from the bitterly cold weather of the Ice Ages.

The seals, sealions and walrus have often been grouped separately from the Carnivora, in a distinct order, the Pinnipedia. They were believed to have evolved independently of terrestrial carnivores, or perhaps from two separate sources, the weasels and bears. However, recent studies have shown that these marine carnivores branched from the main caniform line once only, in the Late Oligocene or Early Miocene.

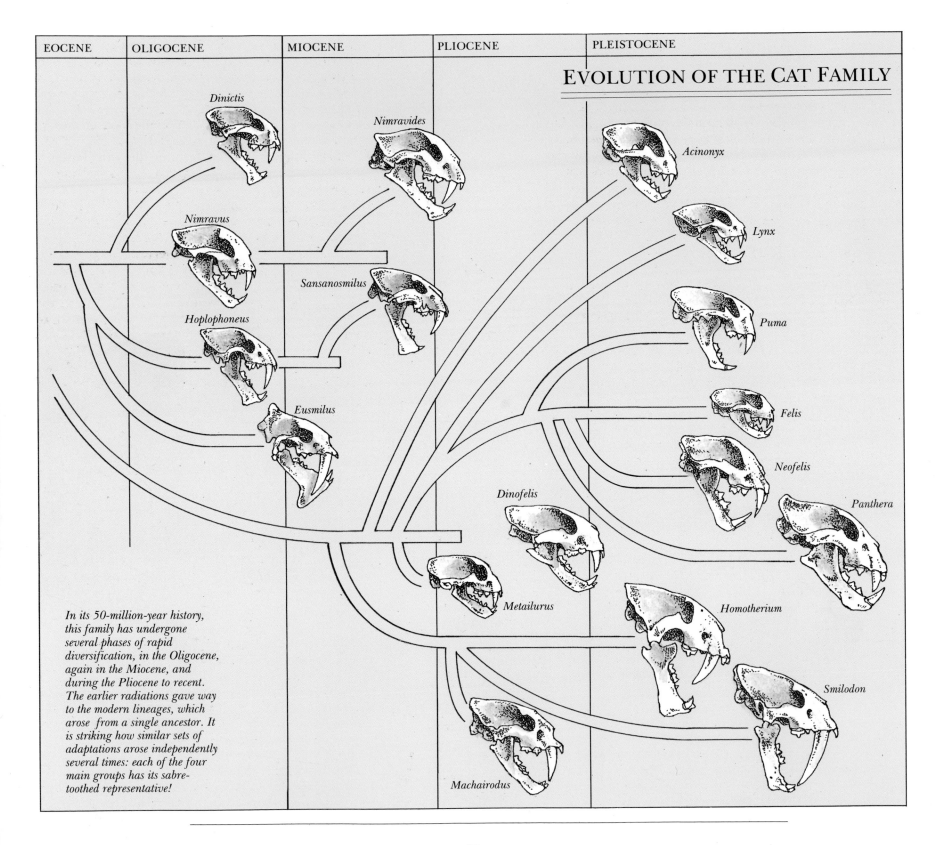

EOCENE	OLIGOCENE	MIOCENE	PLIOCENE	PLEISTOCENE

EVOLUTION OF THE CAT FAMILY

Dinictis

Nimravides

Acinonyx

Nimravus

Lynx

Sansanosmilus

Hoplophoneus

Puma

Eusmilus

Felis

Neofelis

Panthera

Dinofelis

Metailurus

Homotherium

Smilodon

Machairodus

In its 50-million-year history, this family has undergone several phases of rapid diversification, in the Oligocene, again in the Miocene, and during the Pliocene to recent. The earlier radiations gave way to the modern lineages, which arose from a single ancestor. It is striking how similar sets of adaptations arose independently several times: each of the four main groups has its sabre-toothed representative!

Fossils of the first seal-like animals, such as *Enaliarctos* from the Early Miocene rock formations of California, USA, reveal they had short skulls with big eyes, and a poor sense of smell. *Enaliarctos* probably looked like a large otter, with flipper-like limbs and a short tail. It had typical carnivore teeth, but later seals acquired a much simplified dentition with a row of identical peg-like teeth. *Allodesmus*, also from the Early Miocene of California, USA, was larger, at 2 metres (more than 6 feet) long. This more seal-like creature had broad paddle-shaped flippers, a very small tail and large eyes, and its skull cavities indicate some ability to detect the direction of sound underwater.

Mammals take to the air

The bats are classified in the mammalian order Chiroptera and include about 1,000 species today – one-quarter of all living mammals. The reason for their spectacular success is their flying ability and the skill of most species in hunting insects at night. The bats fall into two groups: the large fruit bats, and the smaller and much more diverse insect-eating forms. The oldest fossil bat remains date from the Late Palaeocene, but complete skeletons are known only from the Early Eocene onwards.

An example of an early bat is *Icaronycteris* from the Green River Formation of Wyoming USA. These rocks are famous for the exceptional preservation of fishes, in particular. Other well-preserved bats of similar age are known from the Messel oil shales (see page 55). The skeleton of *Icaronycteris* gives little indication of the ancestry of the bats, since it is already well-evolved and essentially modern in most features: the arm was very long; the second to fifth fingers were spread out to support the flight membrane, which was made from skin; the shoulder girdle was modified to take the huge flight muscles; and the feet could turn backwards, allowing *Icaronycteris* to hang upside down as modern bats do.

In the skull, the braincase was large, as were the eye sockets. The ear region shows evidence of echolocation, the sonar-type technique used by modern bats to detect objects in the dark. High-pitched squeaks are emitted from the mouth and nose region, and their echoes give the bat a precise "sound picture" of what lies ahead.

The only primitive features seen in *Icaronycteris* are its unfused ribs, some features of the fingers, and the retention of certain teeth which are absent in modern bats.

NIPPERS AND STABBERS

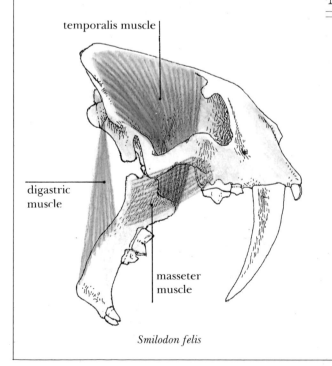

temporalis muscle

digastric muscle

masseter muscle

Smilodon felis

The sabre-tooth type of cat skull involves major changes in the shape and mobility of the lower jaw, and in the relative size of the canine teeth. The jaw action was highly specialized compared to more typical cats. A modern cat uses its canine teeth for stabbing at prey, its incisors for nipping off flesh, and its cheek teeth for tearing tough flesh and shearing gristle and bone. In sabre-tooths, the main jaw movement was the "pincer stab", when the canines stabbed and punched through the thick skin of the prey, and then the jaws closed to lever out a chunk of flesh. The masseter muscle could relax and allow the lower jaw to drop, so that the sabre-toothed cat had an enormously wide gape.

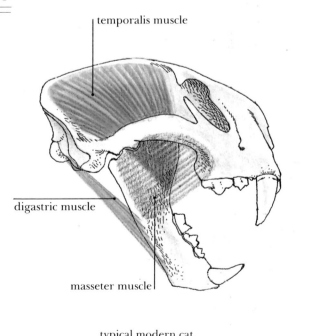

temporalis muscle

digastric muscle

masseter muscle

typical modern cat

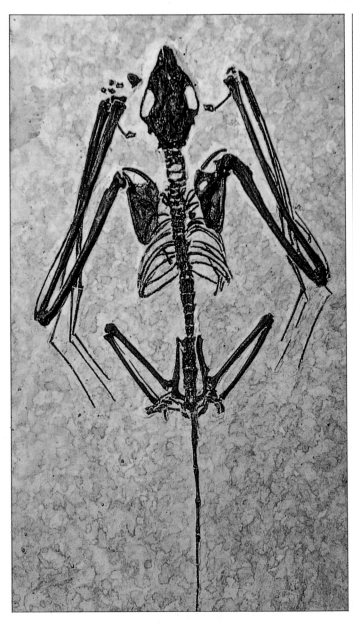

Bats are rare as fossils, since their bones are thin and fragile, but some finds have been spectacularly well preserved. One of the oldest bats, Icaronycteris (left), is known from several exquisite specimens found in the Green River Formation (Early Eocene) of Wyoming. The large eyes and long tail are clearly visible, as are the needle-thin fingers that supported the wing membrane. A slightly younger bat, Palaeochiropteryx from the Middle Eocene Messel deposit (below), shows similar fine detail. There is also evidence of soft tissues and even the thin wing membranes.

and the modern monkeys and apes began to diversify in the Oligocene and Miocene epochs. For a long time, primate evolution has been linked to that of the insectivores, but their true affinities are now believed to lie with the bats and tree shrews. This new view is based on the structure of the ankle, and the presence in males of a "pendulous penis suspended by a reduced sheath between the genital pouch and the abdomen"!

The tree shrews of the order Scandentia are a small group that lives in South-East Asia, feeding on insects and fruit. They resemble a cross between a shrew and a squirrel, although they are truly in neither group, and they have often been placed between the Insectivora and the Primates as evolutionary intermediaries. However, their true affinities seem to lie with the Archonta.

The fourth archontan group, the flying lemurs, are classified as the mammalian order Dermoptera. There is only one living genus, the colugo of South-East Asia. The

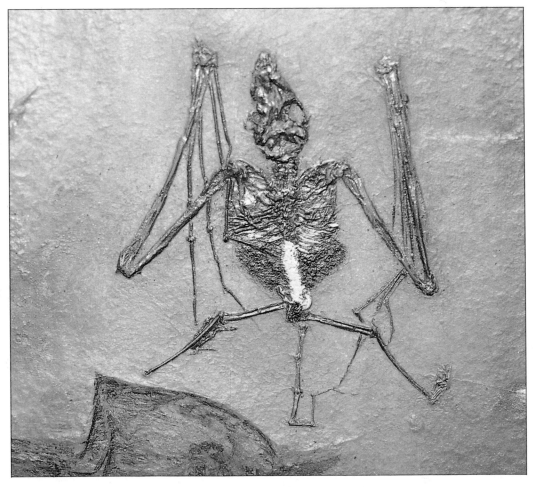

Airborne lemurs and shrews in trees

Relatives of the bats include the primates, the tree shrews and the flying lemurs; these four orders are grouped as the superorder Archonta.

The order Primates contains the living lemurs, monkeys, apes and humans. In fact it was one of the first modern mammalian orders to come on the scene, possibly in the last part of the Cretaceous period. Various primitive primates, some rather like modern bushbabies and lemurs, are known from the Palaeocene and Eocene,

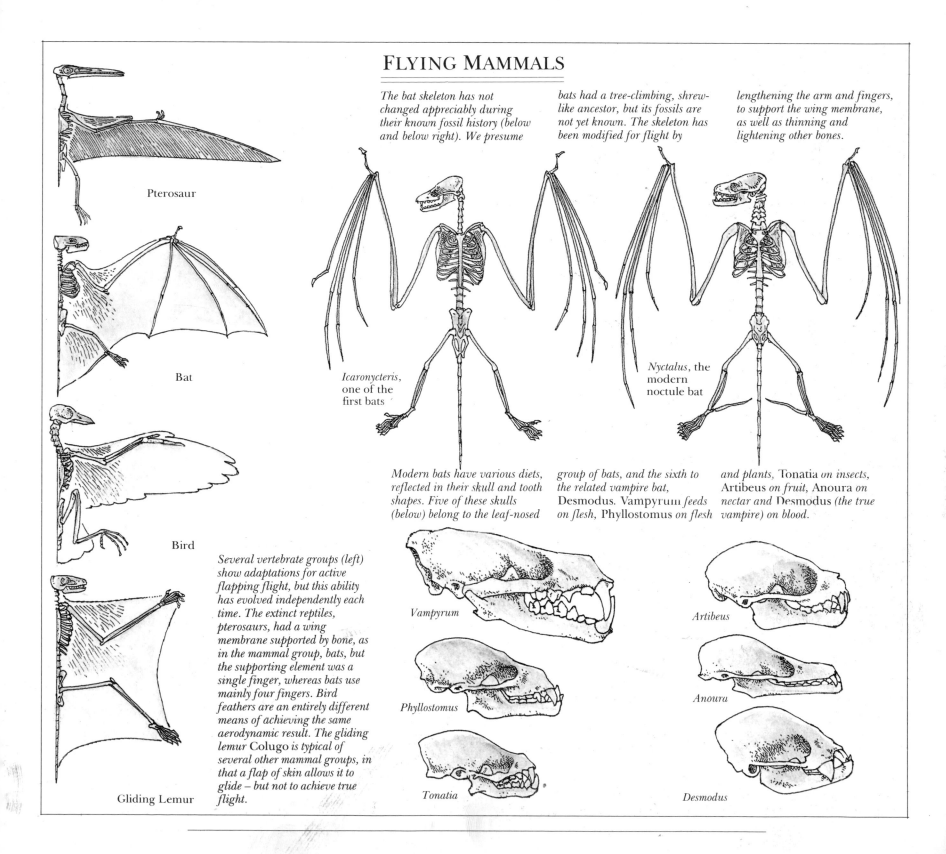

FLYING MAMMALS

The bat skeleton has not changed appreciably during their known fossil history (below and below right). We presume bats had a tree-climbing, shrew-like ancestor, but its fossils are not yet known. The skeleton has been modified for flight by lengthening the arm and fingers, to support the wing membrane, as well as thinning and lightening other bones.

Pterosaur

Bat

Bird

Gliding Lemur

Icaronycteris, one of the first bats

Nyctalus, the modern noctule bat

Modern bats have various diets, reflected in their skull and tooth shapes. Five of these skulls (below) belong to the leaf-nosed group of bats, and the sixth to the related vampire bat, Desmodus. Vampyrum *feeds on flesh,* Phyllostomus *on flesh and plants,* Tonatia *on insects,* Artibeus *on fruit,* Anoura *on nectar and* Desmodus *(the true vampire) on blood.*

Several vertebrate groups (left) show adaptations for active flapping flight, but this ability has evolved independently each time. The extinct reptiles, pterosaurs, had a wing membrane supported by bone, as in the mammal group, bats, but the supporting element was a single finger, whereas bats use mainly four fingers. Bird feathers are an entirely different means of achieving the same aerodynamic result. The gliding lemur Colugo *is typical of several other mammal groups, in that a flap of skin allows it to glide – but not to achieve true flight.*

Vampyrum

Phyllostomus

Tonatia

Artibeus

Anoura

Desmodus

colugo has a long-limbed skeleton that is adapted for tree-climbing, and there is a membrane of skin stretched between the legs, body and tail, that is used for gliding. The colugo can launch itself from the tree tops and leap for distances up to 100 metres (330 feet). Fossil records are scanty, but possible early dermopterans have been reported from Palaeocene and Eocene remains in North America.

The success of the gnawers

The most successful order of mammals is the rodents (Rodentia). Their 1,700 species make up two-fifths of all living mammals. They seem to be infinitely adaptable, as shown by the way in which mice, rats and squirrels have modified their lifestyles to live in close association with humans, even in their houses and cities.

The success of the rodents seems to be founded on their remarkable teeth and jaws, which allow them to eat almost anything, even wood and paper. This inexhaustible food supply permits high breeding rates, and so high rates of evolutionary change.

The dominant feature of rodent dentition is the pair of continuously-growing incisor teeth in both upper and lower jaws. These incisors' long roots curve back inside the bones of the skull above and over the snout to the eye socket, and below into virtually the entire length of the lower jaw. Unusually, the roots are open, and these teeth grow continuously like our finger nails, rather than stopping at a fixed size as in nearly all other mammals. The incisors are triangular in cross section, and they bear hard enamel only on the front surface. As the softer underlying dentine behind the enamel wears faster, it produces a chisel-like enamel cutting edge at the front.

Behind the incisors is a long gap, the diastema, as seen in other herbivores (see page 30), which is followed by four cheek teeth. These have a variety of structural patterns,

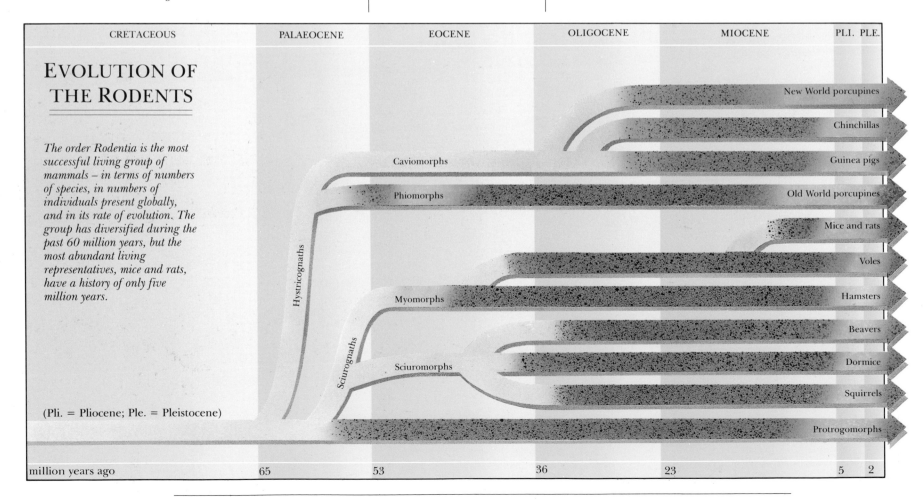

EVOLUTION OF THE RODENTS

The order Rodentia is the most successful living group of mammals – in terms of numbers of species, in numbers of individuals present globally, and in its rate of evolution. The group has diversified during the past 60 million years, but the most abundant living representatives, mice and rats, have a history of only five million years.

(Pli. = Pliocene; Ple. = Pleistocene)

CRETACEOUS | PALAEOCENE | EOCENE | OLIGOCENE | MIOCENE | PLI. PLE.

New World porcupines
Chinchillas
Caviomorphs
Guinea pigs
Phiomorphs
Old World porcupines
Mice and rats
Hystricognaths
Voles
Myomorphs
Hamsters
Beavers
Sciurognaths
Sciuromorphs
Dormice
Squirrels
Protrogomorphs

million years ago | 65 | 53 | 36 | 23 | 5 | 2

depending on diet. Squirrels and mice have multicusped teeth which are used to chew tubers, berries, seeds, nuts and small animals. Voles, lemmings and guinea pigs have high continuously-growing teeth with enamel ridges, for grazing on plants such as sedges and grasses.

When chewing, a rodent pulls its jaws back and forwards in a largely sawing motion. Therefore the two main functions of the teeth – gnawing by the incisors, and chewing by the cheek teeth – cannot occur at the same time. The lower jaw must slide forwards for the incisors to engage, and backwards for the cheek teeth to operate. Two powerful jaw muscles, which cross over each other, produce these movements. These are the pterygoidcus and the masseter muscles, which run respectively from the palate to the back of the lower jaw, and from the back of the skull to the middle of the lower jaw. The different groups of rodents are classified according to the structure of these jaw muscles and the way they work.

The first rodents arose in the Late Palaeocene and Eocene. They were squirrel-like scamperers such as *Paramys* from North America, with a primitive dentition in which the incisors and cheek teeth were not the formidable battery they are today. Later rodent evolution led to some astonishing creatures in the Miocene of the northern hemisphere (see page 120), and in South America some rodents became as large as deer and some as big as rhinoceroses!

Rabbit evolution

The origins and links between rodents and rabbits have been debated for many years, and the idea that the two groups are closely related has gone in and out of favour. It seems to be growing in popularity again at present. Certainly, rabbits have very similar, continuously-growing incisors to the rodents, although rabbits have additional

(Continued on page 76.)

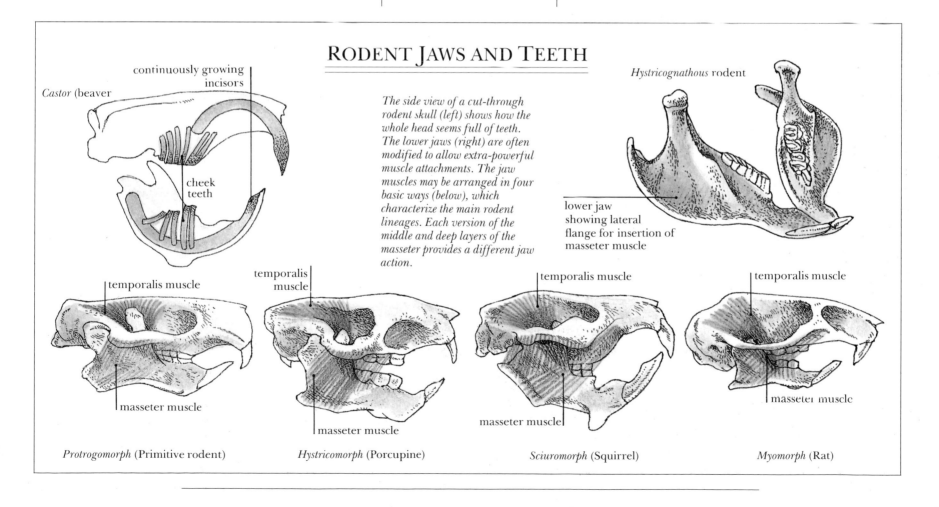

RODENT JAWS AND TEETH

Castor (beaver

continuously growing
incisors

cheek
teeth

The side view of a cut-through rodent skull (left) shows how the whole head seems full of teeth. The lower jaws (right) are often modified to allow extra-powerful muscle attachments. The jaw muscles may be arranged in four basic ways (below), which characterize the main rodent lineages. Each version of the middle and deep layers of the masseter provides a different jaw action.

Hystricognathous rodent

lower jaw
showing lateral
flange for insertion of
masseter muscle

temporalis muscle

masseter muscle

Protrogomorph (Primitive rodent)

temporalis
muscle

masseter muscle

Hystricomorph (Porcupine)

temporalis muscle

masseter muscle

Sciuromorph (Squirrel)

temporalis muscle

masseter muscle

Myomorph (Rat)

ASIA IN THE OLIGOCENE

By Middle Oligocene times, some 30 million years ago, most mammals would seem familiar to us today. This scene from central Asia contains large cats, pigs and a rabbit, along with small insectivores and tree-dwellers. Less familiar are extinct forms such as the later creodonts (close to the ancestry of modern carnivores), and a giant hornless rhinoceros. The Oligocene climate was less humid and tropical than in the Eocene. For the first time, large areas of arid grasslands spread across many parts of the world, and some animals ventured out of the protective forests to take advantage of the new food sources. This stimulated adaptations for fast running, rather than camouflage.

The world as it was then.

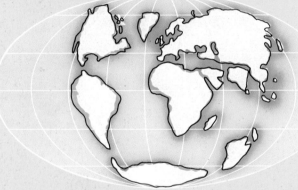

The Oligocene mammals of Asia ranged greatly in size, from small cats such as Nimravus (2) and the rabbit Ordolagus (3), to the creodont Hyaenodon (1).

The monstrous Indricotherium *(4) was 5.4 metres (18 feet) tall, and the largest land mammal of all time. The pig* Entelodon *(5) was 2 metres (nearly 7 feet) long.*

smaller incisors behind the front pair.

An early rabbit is *Palaeolagus* from Oligocene times in North America. It probably looked little different from a modern rabbit, with a short tail, long hind limbs, and strong limb girdles; these features show that it moved by hopping. The teeth indicate that it fed on grass and leaves, which it nipped off with the incisors and chewed with the cheek teeth.

A small mammalian order, the Macroscelidea – the "elephant shrews" of Africa – may be associated with the rabbits and rodents. The oldest fossil elephant shrews are Oligocene in age. Their study shows that these early representatives had a long flexible snout, used to hunt for insects, and they moved by hopping on their long, thin hind limbs.

On the hoof

There were few large plant-eaters in Palaeocene times, other than the uintatheres (see page 49). Other herbivores were generally no larger than sheep. But new hoofed plant-eaters appeared in the Eocene, possibly from among the "condylarths". They split into the two groups we know today: the odd-toed ungulates, the order Perissodactyla, with one, three or five toes; and the even-toed ungulates, order Artiodactyla, with two or four toes on each foot. The perissodactyls rose to prominence first, and the early forms include ancestors of the living horses, tapirs and rhinoceroses.

The first horse, *Hyracotherium*, was an inconspicuous animal that browsed on the leaves of low bushes during the Eocene epoch of Europe and North America. *Hyracotherium* was a small animal, about the size of a terrier, with four toes on its fore-foot and three on its hind. Its teeth

The ancient rabbit Palaeolagus haydeni *from the Middle Oligocene Brule Formation of the South Dakota Badlands, USA. Rabbits are not rodents but lagomorphs, and although the skull is superficially rodent-like, it differs in having a small second incisor in the upper jaw, just behind the main one. (Rodents have only one incisor on each side.) Also lagomorphs have more than the five cheek teeth possessed by rodents.* Palaeolagus *had the powerful jaws of living rabbits, and fed on tough grass. We assume it also had long ears to improve its hearing ability, but fossils cannot show this!*

Amynodon *was representative of the amynodonts, an early branch of the rhino group that was abundant in the Late Eocene and Early Oligocene of North America and Asia. The canine teeth are still large, as in more primitive groups, and the skull is very short. The massive grinding molars indicate a diet of tough vegetation. The amynodonts have been variously classified as rhinos or tapirs.*

were low and its jaws shallow, since the leaves which it ate were not a demanding diet. (It is sometimes called *Eohippus*.)

During the Oligocene, horses became larger. *Mesohippus* was the size of a sheep and had three toes on each foot, with the middle toe rather larger than the other two. The snout was longer than in *Hyracotherium*, and the teeth and jaws were deeper. It seems that *Mesohippus* and its Oligocene relatives were adapted for life in open woodlands and savannah grasslands, feeding on a mixed diet of leaves and grasses.

The story of horse evolution continued through the Miocene, and it has become a classic example of an evolutionary trend, where a whole range of characters seem to be changing in a certain way through time. The story is taken up again on page 105.

Rhinos through the ages

The tapirs of Central and South America and the rhinoceroses of India and Africa are probably related. Both groups can be traced back to Eocene ancestors in North America. Living tapirs browse on leaves in tropical forests, a mode of life not unlike that of the earliest perissodactyls. The rhinoceroses have had a more dramatic evolutionary story.

The first known rhinos were sheep-sized running animals which lacked the characteristic nose horns. However, some giant forms arose in the Oligocene. *Indricotherium* from Asia was the largest land mammal of all

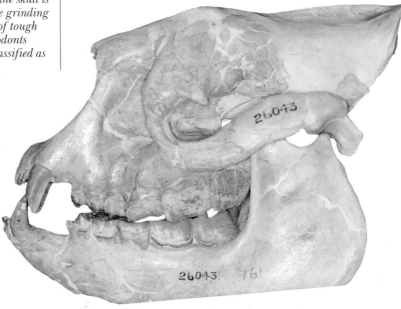

BRONTOTHERIUM

The brontotheres, or titanotheres, were abundant animals in the early Tertiary of North America and eastern Asia. They seem to have acted as "rhinoceros substitutes". Brontotherium itself stood 2.5 metres (8 feet) tall at the shoulder. The vast catapult-like horn was probably used in courtship or rivalry displays, and in defence; the massive shoulders attest to powerful butting and wrestling abilities. Brontotheres fed on soft vegetation, and they died out in the Late Oligocene as tough grasses spread over the dry plains.

time, standing 5.4 metres (18 feet) high at the shoulder, and weighing about 30 tonnes (32 tons) – five times as much as a large elephant! This giant could feed on leaves from tall trees, but its group died out in the Miocene.

The horned rhinos then evolved rapidly in the Miocene and Pliocene, to include the woolly rhino, *Coelodonta*, of the Pleistocene ice ages (see page 131). The rhinoceros horn, mistakenly reputed to be an aphrodisiac today, is not made from horn or bone, but from tightly fused, matted hair.

An unusual perissodactyl side-branch in the Oligocene were the brontotheres or titanotheres, which looked superficially like the earlier uintatheres. *Brontotherium* from the Early Oligocene of North America was a heavily-built animal, 2.5 metres (8 feet) tall at the shoulder, and equipped with a curious branched horn on its snout that looked like a thickened catapult. In life, the horn was probably covered with skin, and it may have been used in dominance displays or fighting for mates. The brontotheres died out in the Mid Oligocene, and they were replaced ecologically by the giant rhinos.

Prehistoric pigs

The second main ungulate group, the even-toed forms of

the order Artiodactyla, fall into two groups: pigs and hippos on one hand, and cattle, deer, giraffes, camels and antelopes on the other. Artiodactyls arose in the Early Eocene, and the first representatives were slender rabbit-sized animals that fed on leaves. Major adaptive radiations of artiodactyls occurred in the Late Eocene and Oligocene.

The first evolutionary burst involved the oreodonts, such as *Merycoidodon*, in North America. These were low, short-limbed, pig-sized animals with four toes on each foot. They had the typical selenodont, literally "moon-teeth", pattern of cusps on their cheek teeth, as seen in all artiodactyls except the pigs and hippos. The cusps form pairs of ridges resembling crescents or moons, and these were effective and durable grinders. Skeletons of *Merycoidodon* and other oreodonts are so common in the Late Oligocene rocks of the South Dakota Badlands in the USA

Trigonias, one of the first true rhinos, lived during Early Oligocene times in North America. The skull is longer than in Amynodon *(see page 76), but the beast probably did not look much like a modern rhino.* Trigonias *was the size of a small pony, and like many prehistoric rhinos it lacked a horn; it probably resembled a small, stocky, hairless horse.*

that they are called the Oreodon Beds.

Agriochoerus was a contemporary of *Merycoidodon*, similar in many respects, but with claws instead of hooves on its feet. It may have moved about in the low branches of trees, stripping them of succulent leaves and berries.

Walking on two toes

A modern group that arose from these kings of artiodactyls is the camels and llamas. *Poebrotherium*, a camel from the Oligocene of North America, was a slender, goat-sized animal. Like all camels, it had a long neck, long limbs, and three of its toes on each foot had virtually disappeared. *Poebrotherium* walked on the two middle toes (numbers three and four) which splayed slightly, and it was clearly an animal that could range with great speed over wide savannah grasslands. The camels, and their relatives the cattle and deer, became very important in the Miocene.

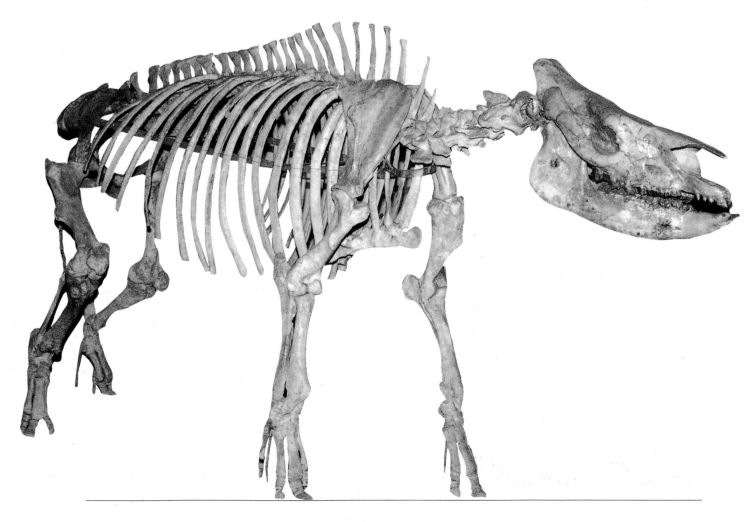

MERYCOIDODON

One of the commonest mammals on the plains of North America in Late Oligocene times was Merycoidodon – *a typical oreodont, a primitive relative of pigs and camels. This short-legged, sheep-sized animal grazed the early grasses in huge herds. It is not clear why the group went extinct – especially when we consider its numbers in the "Oreodon Beds", where thousands of* Merycoidodon *skeletons lie out in the Badlands of South Dakota.*

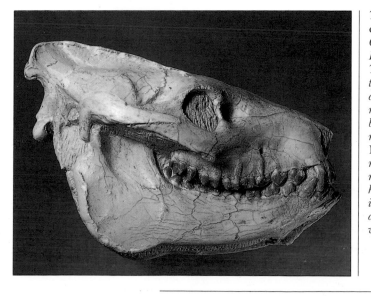

The skull of Merycoidodon culbertsonii *from the Middle Oligocene Brule Formation of the Big Badlands, South Dakota. The deep, hatchet-shaped jaw is typical of grazing ungulates: it accommodates the deeply-rooted molar cheek teeth and provides broad anchorage for the chewing masseter and temporalis muscles.* Merycoidodon *was probably more of an omnivore than modern ungulates, since it still had well developed canines and incisors, which would have allowed it to cope with a wide variety of foods.*

The pig-hippo group of artiodactyls evolved and spread from Late Eocene times onwards, but it never achieved the diversity or abundance of the selenodont artiodactyls. The ancestors of modern pigs, peccaries and hippos can be traced back to the Oligocene and Miocene. During the Oligocene, North America was populated by giant pig-like animals such as *Entelodon*, which was up to 3 metres (10 feet) long. Its heavy, lengthened skull had a generalized dentition that could indicate a diet of water-side plants, as well as meat. It is therefore possible that pigs have always been omnivores, able to eat almost anything.

Mammals take to the sea

The whales and dolphins (mammalian order Cetacea) include the largest animal of all time, the living 30-metre

(100-feet) long blue whale. Modern whales and dolphins seem to be so well adapted to life in the water – with their fast and efficient swimming, their diet of fishes, molluscs and krill, and their ability to dive to immense depths while holding their breath – that it may be hard to accept that they arose from terrestrial ancestors.

The oldest known whale is *Pakicetus*, an incompletely preserved animal from the Early Eocene rocks of Pakis-

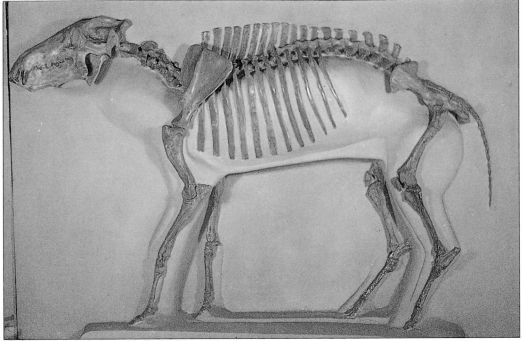

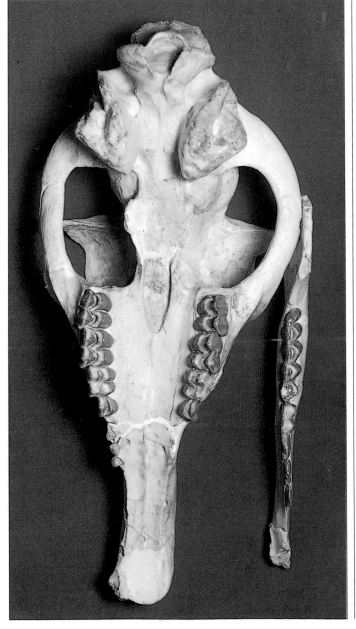

Archaeotherium was a large, pig-like animal from the Middle Oligocene Brule Formation of the Big Badlands, South Dakota (above). This long-limbed animal could run faster than modern pigs. The long skull bears various bony excrescences of unknown function.

The skull of Poebrotherium *(left), an early camel from the Middle Oligocene Brule Formation of Scenic, South Dakota. This view shows the palate (roof of the mouth) and one half of the lower jaw, and highlights the arrangement and wear patterns of the teeth. The cheek teeth have crescent-shaped cusps from rasping plant food. The crescent or moon shape is typical of most artiodactyls (even-toed ungulates) and is termed selenodont ("moon-toothed").*

tan. The skull had a long snout lined with primitive carnivorous teeth, which are hard to distinguish from those of the mesonychids (see page 50). Thus, it seems that whales did indeed descend from these early land carnivores, and moved into the water in search of new prey. The skeleton of *Pakicetus* is not known, but indications are that it was probably rather like that of a large otter. This early whale would have had broad, paddle-like hands and feet and a bulky streamlined body, and was still able to come onto land.

By Late Eocene times, whales were fully marine and had lost most traces of their former terrestrial existence. One of the most dramatic members was *Basilosaurus*, first found in the 1830s (see page 12). It was 20 metres (66 feet) long, with the slender body of a mythical sea serpent! The head was relatively small, being about one-fifteenth of the total length, compared to one-quarter or one-third in modern whales. The teeth were triangular and pointed, as in *Pakicetus*, and their edges were lined with small, pointed cusps. The long serpentine body would undulate to provide swimming thrust, with front paddles for rudders. The hind limbs were reduced to small splints of bone entirely within the body.

After the Eocene, the whales developed into two main groups: the toothed dolphins, porpoises and sperm whales, and the whalebone or baleen whales. All the larger species are baleen whales, in which the teeth have disappeared. Instead, the mouth contains strips of baleen, a tough and stringy substance akin to horn. Fossils of toothed, dolphin-like whales are best known, with dozens of specimens having been found from the Miocene epoch.

From old to new

On land, and in the sea, the Oligocene epoch marked a turning point in mammalian evolution. Most of the Palaeocene and Eocene groups were disappearing, and the modern mammalian orders were evolving rapidly. The Miocene and Pliocene epochs (24–2 million years ago) were to see the full flowering of some of these modern groups, as described in chapter five.

The skull of the primitive whale Dorudon, *a relative of* Basilosaurus, *from the Late Eocene rocks of North America and North Africa. In life,* Dorudon *was more like a porpoise and much smaller than its giant cousin.*

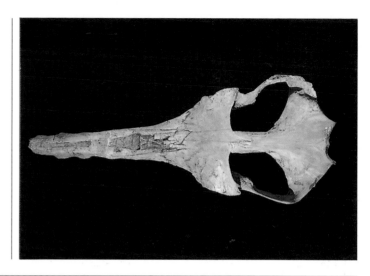

BASILOSAURUS

This early whale bore an uncanny resemblance to a sea serpent, with its long, snake-like body and tiny head in great contrast to the bulky, thick-set body and large head of a modern whale. At lengths of 20-25 metres (65–80 feet), Basilosaurus *was the largest mammal around at the time. It swam by arching its body, and used its large paddles for steering. New specimens brought to light in 1990 show that the rudimentary hind limbs, which no longer served any function, contained all the bones of fully-developed legs – but much reduced in size.*

MARINE MAMMALS

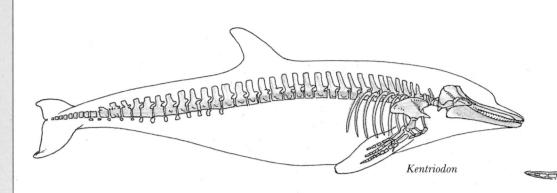

Kentriodon

After the demise of the marine reptiles, several groups of mammals soon became adapted to life in the sea. The most obvious are the whales and dolphins, and the seals and sealions. However, others include the dugongs and seacows, and the sea otters. Whales apparently developed from mesonychid carnivores in the Late Palaeocene, and the Late Eocene whale *Basilosaurus* already showed the key feature of huge size. A recent study showed that *Basilosaurus* still retained its hind limbs, as tiny, useless remnants (vestiges), thus proving that it evolved from a land animal. Toothed whales, such as sperm whales and dolphins, split away from the baleen (whalebone) group during the Oligocene epoch. Seals and sealions appeared at about this time, too.

Fossil beds of the east and west coasts of North America have produced many remains of marine mammals from the Miocene epoch. The early dolphin Kentriodon *(above), from Maryland, is little different from modern species. However,* Allodesmus *(below) from the Pacific coast, although* superficially like a sealion, did in fact belong to an extinct group, the desmatophocids. These had large eyes and primitive ears, while modern sealions have tiny eyes and ears specialized for hunting underwater.

Miocene marine mammals. The dolphin Kentriodon *(5) and the sealion* Allodesmus *(7) were both about 2 metres (nearly 7 feet) long, much larger than the "sea otter"* Potamotherium *(4) and the sealion* Enaliarctos *(6).*

All of these mammals were dwarfed by the huge Basilosaurus *(2), the earliest well-known whale, at 20 metres (about 65 feet) long. Similar in size to* Basilosaurus *are* Balaena *(1) and* Physeter *(3).*

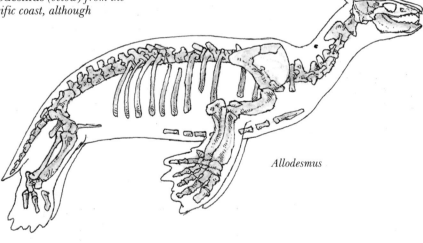

Allodesmus

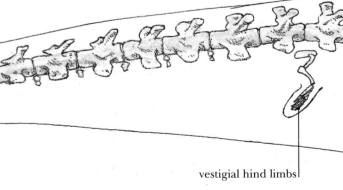

vestigial hind limbs

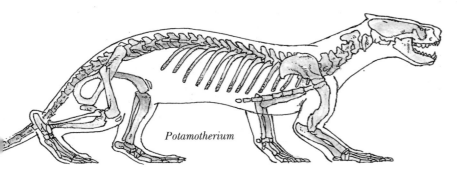

Potamotherium

"Telescoping" in whale skull evolution (right). The primitive pattern, as seen in Zygorhiza from the Late Eocene of the USA, gradually became much modified. In a Miocene toothed whale such as Squalodon, the nostril had moved back over the eyes, and the bones of the snout covered much of the skull roof. This telescoping was produced by rearward migration of the nostril, and it was also associated with the development of an echolocation system.

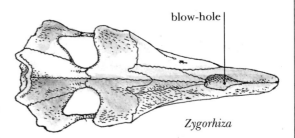

blow-hole

Zygorhiza

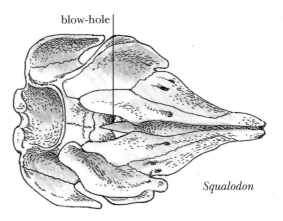

blow-hole

Squalodon

Potamotherium (*above*) and Enaliarctos (*below*) were discovered in Early Miocene rocks in France and on the Pacific coast of the USA, respectively. They appear to be close to the ancestry of sealions. Both were small, terrestrial animals with aquatic adaptations. Potamotherium may be a sea otter or a sealion, while Enaliarctos had crossed the divide and was clearly a sealion.

Enaliarctos

Skeletons of giant whales (below). Modern whales fall into two groups. One contains the toothed whales such as dolphins, porpoises, killer whales, and the largest, the sperm whale Physeter. *The other whale group is the baleen (whalebone) whales; including* Balaena, *the right whale. In both groups the head is relatively huge, to permit feeding on large quantities of small prey: squid and krill respectively. Note the difference in proportions when compared to* Basilosaurus (*bottom*), *which had a relatively small skull.*

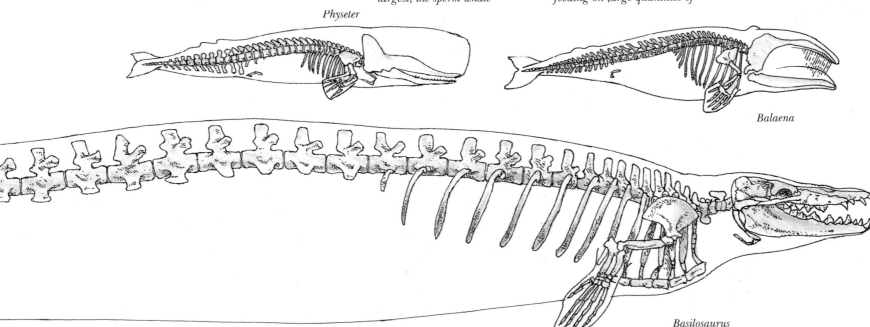

Physeter

Balaena

Basilosaurus

CHAPTER FOUR

THE ISLAND CONTINENTS

The evolution of the mammals during the past 65 million years followed a very different course on the island continents of Australia and South America, compared to the rest of the world. Although South America is now joined to North America, and there has been some spreading of animals across the Panama Isthmus between them, this was not always the case. Until three million years ago, South America was an island. Its animals evolved into unique forms not seen anywhere else in the world. There are, however, close parallels between the mammals of South America and those of the other great island continent, Australia.

South America and Australia share the unusual feature that many of the dominant mammals have been marsupials, rather than the more familiar placentals seen elsewhere. Indeed, at one time, the marsupials were just as important worldwide as the placentals, and it may well have been chance extinctions that have gradually restricted them to their modern distributions. The marsupials arose at the same time as the placentals, in the Early to mid Cretaceous, some 100 million years ago (see page 38).

The first marsupials

The oldest remains of marsupials are isolated jaw fragments, and 30 or more species have been recognized from the Late Cretaceous, in particular from North America. *Alphadon* was a typical example which probably looked rather like the living opossum. Unfortunately, complete skeletons are not known, but these would doubtless show some obvious marsupial characters such as the pair of small

Details of the skull and front part of the skeleton of the giant armoured armadillo Glyptodon, *a Pleistocene creature from South America (opposite). The broad skull had vast bony plates on either side and toothless jaws. The armour even included a bony "toupee" which fitted into the notch on the front of the carapace (body shell), when* Glyptodon *pulled in its head. The armour is made from numerous fused hexagonal plates of bone which grew in the skin, and it provided effective protection from the sabre-toothed "cats" of the time.*

bones in the lower belly region that help to support the pouch. These bones are seen in some other extinct groups of Mesozoic mammals, showing that the pouch which gives marsupials their name was an early and primitive characteristic of these animals.

Alphadon is identified as a marsupial from its teeth: it had three premolars and four molars, whereas placental mammals have four or five premolars and three molars. Other features of the teeth also indicate that *Alphadon* was a marsupial. The upper molars were not as wide for their length as typical placental molars, and they had several large cusps. Two specific pointed cusps in the lower molar were very close together, whereas in placentals these two projections are spaced well apart.

New clues for an old establishment

The Late Cretaceous marsupials of North America are classified into three families, and fossils reveal that these made up nearly half of the species in their animal communities. But for the mass extinction at the end of the Cretaceous, which wiped out two of these three families, as well as the dinosaurs and other groups, the marsupials might well have been even more successful in the Early Palaeocene (see page 42).

In South America, Late Cretaceous marsupials appear to have been even more diverse, with members of five families being reported from Argentina, Peru and Bolivia. Until recently, however, the fossil record gave almost no clues about the crucial episode, some 100-65 million years ago, when all of the unique South American groups became established.

CONTINENTAL DRIFT

There is strong evidence that the surface of the Earth is in constant motion. At the beginning of the Age of Mammals, in the Palaeocene and Eocene epochs, there were land connections from South America to Antarctica and *Australia, which allowed migrations of marsupials. For much of the time, however, South America and Africa were islands, which allowed many unusual groups to evolve in isolation.*

PALAEOCENE

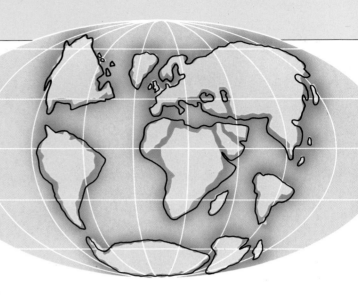

EOCENE

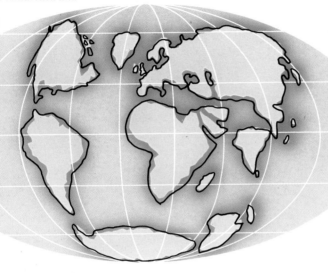

OLIGOCENE

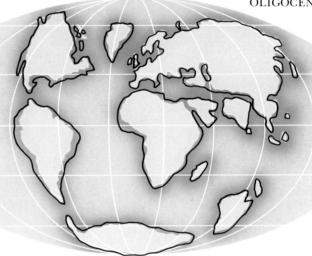

MIOCENE

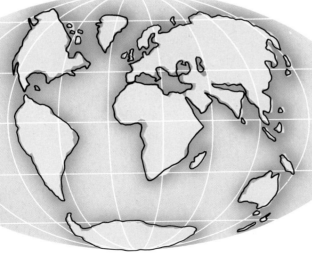

PLIOCENE

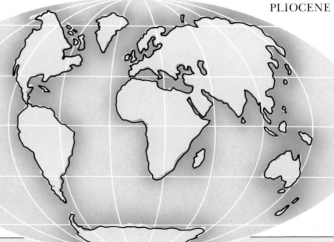

The sole Cretaceous remains consisted of a few jaw fragments from Peru and Argentina, probably those of an opossum, a "condylarth" (see page 48) and a notoungulate (see page 99); the first two of these indicate links with North America.

For much of the Mesozoic era (245-65 million years ago), South America was linked to Africa. But this connection was lost as the South Atlantic Ocean opened up during the Cretaceous period. There may have been a land bridge for a relatively short time between North-Central and South America, about 75 million years ago. This would have allowed the passage of mammals both ways, including the opossums, or didelphids, known from both North and South America in the Late Cretaceous. However, South America seems to have been an island for most of the 65 million years of the Tertiary period, until the formation of the present Isthmus of Panama some three million years ago.

New finds of Late Cretaceous marsupials are now being made with great regularity in South America. Paleontologists have only recently begun to devote attention to collecting such specimens, and no doubt many exciting discoveries will be made in the next few years. Teams of paleontologists from Argentina, France and the USA have identified three major rock deposits in Argentina and Bolivia, that have produced hundreds of good specimens since only 1985.

The two Argentinian localities, dated as Early and Late Cretaceous (about 125 and 75 million years ago respectively), have yielded remains of relatives of the earlier Jurassic groups to the north, such as dryolestids. In addition, there are two or three other families, as well as some specimens unique to South America.

The Bolivian finds include more than 600 specimens of 18 species of marsupials and placentals, mainly teeth. This may not seem like a major discovery at first sight. However, these remains have increased the experts' knowledge of South American Mesozoic mammals immeasurably, since even a single tooth can provide a great deal of information about all aspects of how mammals related to each other, what they ate, and how they lived.

The dominant marsupials in the latest Cretaceous remains from Bolivia are opossums, small insectivores, and omnivores such as *Roberthoffstetteria*, which was a little larger than a rat. Its four molars prove its marsupial nature. The associated placental mammals include two insectivorous animals like *Zalambdalestes* from Mongolia

MAMMALIAN BIRTH CYCLES

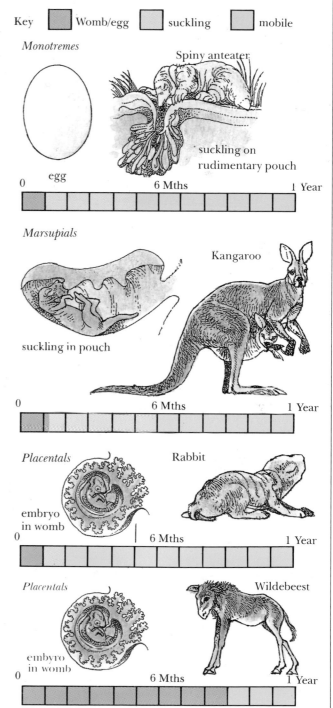

The monotremes have a primitive mammalian method of reproduction, namely egg-laying. This was probably typical of the Mesozoic mammals and the ancestral mammal-like reptiles. The embryo develops inside an egg, which is laid about 15 days after mating. The young hatch, and suck at milk-secreting slits on the mother's abdomen. The youngster's eyes open 15 weeks after hatching, and it is weaned and able to leave the nest at about five months of age.

Marsupials do not lay eggs, but their breeding method is regarded as primitive, since the developing embryo is retained inside the womb for only a short time – a week in small marsupials, or up to 40 days in the larger kangaroos. At birth, the tiny young animal creeps into its mother's pouch, where it sucks at milk-producing teats – for 10 weeks in small species, and up to six months in kangaroos. The young marsupial moves about independently after that, but it often returns to the pouch for milk until it is twice that age.

In the majority of mammals – the placentals – the embryo remains in the mother's womb until it has developed to a relatively advanced state. The length of gestation (pregnancy) is broadly related to body size: 12–20 days in shrews, 8–9 months in wildebeeste and humans, and 21 months in elephants. In many placentals, a similar time span elapses before the young animal is able to move about independently, but in many open-plains species such as the wildebeeste (gnu), the young is able to walk almost immediately after birth, so that it can keep up with the moving herd, even while feeding on milk from its mother.

Key — Womb/egg — suckling — mobile

Monotremes — Spiny anteater — suckling on rudimentary pouch — 0 — egg — 6 Mths — 1 Year

Marsupials — Kangaroo — suckling in pouch — 0 — 6 Mths — 1 Year

Placentals — Rabbit — embryo in womb — 0 — 6 Mths — 1 Year

Placentals — Wildebeest — embryo in womb — 0 — 6 Mths — 1 Year

MIGRATION ROUTES

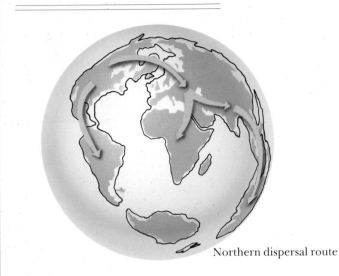

Northern dispersal route

Explaining the present geographical distribution of marsupials, which is centred on Australia and South America, has always been a challenge to biologists. How did these mammals get from one continent to the other? Until recently, paleontologists had to favour the theory of a northern dispersal route, with marsupials moving north through the Americas, over Greenland to Europe, and then through Asia to Australasia. However, recent evidence now shows that South America was formerly in contact with Australia via Antarctica, and marsupials have been found in that southernmost continent.

Southern dispersal route

(see page 39), three omnivorous "condylarths", and two herbivores – a pantodont and a notoungulate (see pages 48 and 99). These fossils show clear links with North American contemporaries.

Marsupial migrations

The present split distribution of marsupials between South America and Australia has long puzzled zoologists. In a world dominated by placental mammals, why is it that marsupials survive today only in these regions, with a recent overspill into North America after the formation of the Central American land bridge? Did they swim across the Pacific – or walk over Greenland, Europe, Asia and the Malaysian islands, to reach Australia from North America?

Biogeographers have developed a variety of theories to explain the present distribution of marsupials. The traditionally favoured view was the "northern dispersal route" just outlined. Somehow the early marsupials travelled across the North Atlantic via Arctic land bridges, and then trekked thousands of kilometres south-west across Eurasia towards Australia. The problems with this view were that distances are vast, and fossil marsupials had never been found in Asia!

With the acceptance of the theory of continental drift (see page 26), biogeographers noticed that South America and Australia had formerly been in close contact as parts of the great land mass Pangaea, until about the

The skull of a typical monotreme, the echidna Zaglossus, from Australia and New Guinea. There are only two types of living monotremes, the echidnas (spiny anteaters) and platypus. The group must have had a wider distribution, but fossils have never been found outside Australasia.

beginning of the Cretaceous – some time before the origin of the marsupials. However, as the South Atlantic and Indian Oceans began to open up, a loose connection still existed via the southern tip of South America, now called Tierra del Fuego, to the northern peninsula of Antarctica, and from Antarctica to Australia. Perhaps the marsupials migrated via a "southern dispersal route", from South America across Antarctica (which was not icebound at the time) to Australia, possibly in the Palaeocene or Eocene (65-37 million years ago). The problem with this theory was that marsupial fossils had not been found in Antarctica, either – probably because few people had looked for them there.

Confusingly, recent fossil discoveries have filled both gaps. Fossil marsupials have now been found both in Asia and in Antarctica! How are these to be reconciled with the dispersal routes, unless both occurred?

The fossil record of marsupials, until fairly recently, included a few finds from North America and Europe. It seemed that didelphids (opossums) had passed into Europe in the early Tertiary period, and they survived there until the Miocene (about 20 million years ago). The didelphids had already entered South America during the Late Cretaceous, and they survive there to this day. Marsupials died out in North America in the Miocene, but they reinvaded from South America in the last few thousand years. Even in Australia the fossil record of marsupials is sparse, and it offers few guides to their date of entry to that continent. Only a few odd teeth and jaws were known from the Late Oligocene, with more diverse and abundant remains from the Miocene onwards. At least, this was the situation until the middle of the 1980s, when a whole new range of marsupial fossils came to light.

The southern route wins out

The first find was the incomplete remains of a polydolopid marsupial from the Eocene of Antarctica, found by an American research team. The polydolopids are a South American group of marsupials, and they could have wandered freely on to Antarctica, which (as mentioned above) was not ice-covered at that time. The date of the fossil, Eocene, fits the evidence that the marsupials reached Australia by the southern route during the Oligocene.

The next finds were marsupials from Africa; a molar tooth of a didelphid from the Early Eocene of Algeria, and three jaw fragments from Oligocene rocks in northern Egypt. These specimens were all virtually the same as European marsupials of the same age, and therefore they did not add significantly to the resolution of the "northern or southern" debate. The African finds were important, though, in adding yet another continent to our knowledge of former marsupial distribution.

The third find, made in the late 1980s, was a small marsupial tooth from the Oligocene (about 37 million years ago) of central Asia. It comes from a didelphid rather like the European specimens. If this Asian tooth had been found 40 years ago, it would doubtless have been taken as evidence for the northern trans-Asia route to Australia. The new fossil, however, has no particular Australian affinities, being most like the American-European didelphids. So, like the African finds, it shows how the marsupials spread from Europe into other areas, but there is still no good evidence that marsupials penetrated further across Asia and hence to Australia.

The "southern route" theory seems to have been vindicated, since it fits the paleogeographic evidence best. The recent finds also show how widespread the marsupials once were. Even after their virtual annihilation during the end-of-Cretaceous extinction (see page 42), they recovered sufficiently to achieve a worldwide distribution in the Eocene and Oligocene, although only as small, tree-climbing insectivores. Nevertheless, our contemporary view is rather different from the traditional one, which emphasized how unsuccessful the marsupials were in comparison with the placentals.

The skulls of monotremes are rather odd-looking. Two platypus skulls (right) – the large one being Obdurodon *from the Miocene, and the smaller, the living platypus* Ornithorhynchus *– show the pincer-like bony outline of the duck bill at the top, and the overall long, low shape. The other monotremes, the echidnas such as* Tachyglossus *(below), have long narrow snouts for licking up termites and ants.*

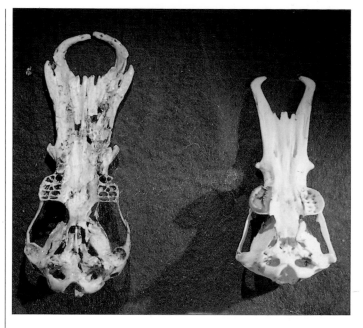

A world apart

Marsupials are the dominant native mammals in Australia, and they have been so since they arrived there some 30 or more million years ago. This has enabled them to achieve great diversity. Some are quite unlike anything elsewhere in the world, while others parallel their placental counterparts from other continents.

However, we should remember that the marsupials were not the first mammals to reach the shores of Australia. The monotremes, the egg-laying platypus and echidna (see page 38) have relatives dating back to the Early Cretaceous, about 120 million years ago. Monotremes today are a very small group, and fossils indicate this has always been the case. In that respect, as well their retention of many "reptilian" features such as egg-laying, they can be called "living fossils".

Until 1985, the oldest monotreme fossils came from the Middle Miocene (about 15 million years ago), which was frustrating to paleontologists who knew that there should be much earlier fossils! Indeed, the prevalent view until then had been that the monotremes were not involved in mainstream mammal evolution at all. They were believed by some experts to have had an entirely separate origin, from the cynodont mammal-like reptiles in the Triassic, and to have a unique history of some 225 million years. Cladistic analyses since 1980 have demonstrated convincingly that the monotremes are indeed closely related to the marsupials and placentals, with a branching-off point

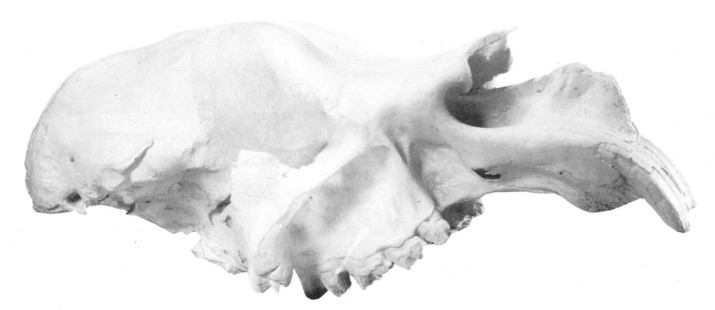

The fossil skull of the giant extinct wombat Diprotodon optatum *(left), from one of the massive Pleistocene bonebeds of southern Australia. It has powerful gnawing incisors at the front, followed by a gap, and then a battery of broad grinding molars at the back. The lower jaw, not shown here, bore a similar long incisor that closed against the upper incisor. The skull is 50 centimetres (20 inches) long.*

possibly in the Late Jurassic. Thus when Early Cretaceous monotreme fossils were found, they neatly filled an embarrassing gap in the fossil record!

Giant kangaroos and wombats

The fossil record of marsupials in Australia begins with rather patchy remains from Oligocene and Early Miocene times. Some remarkably complete remains of unusual animals have been found in the later Miocene, Pliocene and Pleistocene, covering the past 15 million years. The Pleistocene animals are perhaps the most fascinating. Most of these marsupials were like modern ones – only much larger!

The Pleistocene landscape in southern Australia, about one million years ago (see pages 94-95), was dominated by giant wombats, kangaroos and marsupial predators, living alongside giant echidnas and the heavily armoured turtle *Meiolania*. The commonest animal was the giant wombat *Diprotodon*, which was as large as a hippopotamus, and lived in great herds. Indeed, paleontologists have found its bones preserved in spectacular profusion, trapped in rocks formed from lake beds. This gentle giant stood on heavy limbs with broad plantigrade feet (the soles flat on the ground). Its massive skull had powerful jaws, and is essentially a food-processing structure, since *Diprotodon* had rather a small brain. The diprotodonts were a successful Australian group, including a variety of animals, many smaller than *Diprotodon*. They are now totally extinct.

A composite skeleton of the marsupial "lion" Thylacoleo carnifex, *from the Pleistocene rocks of Australia (below). It probably preyed on diprotodonts, although its teeth are not typical of large meat-eaters.*

The giant kangaroos include *Procoptodon*, a short-faced beast which used its powerful jaws to chew grass and tough leaves. Its skull was short and deep, as in *Diprotodon*, rather than long and dog-like as in modern kangaroos. However, like today's kangaroos, *Procoptodon* had four toes on each foot and the fourth (outer) was the only

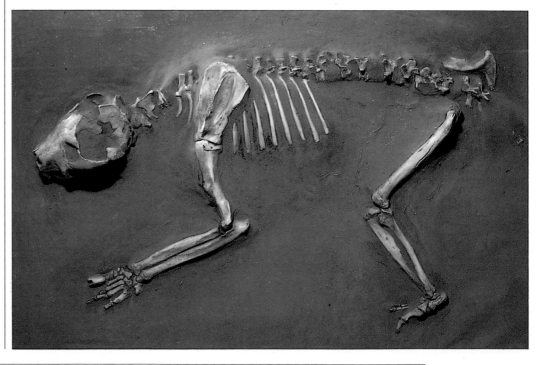

Marsupial hunters

Most of the giant Pleistocene herbivores of Australia could resist predation because of their size. But young, weak or older animals, as well as smaller species, were hunted by the marsupial lion, *Thylacoleo*. This animal had a heavy skull 25 centimetres (10 inches) long, with strong canine-like incisor teeth and exceptionally long blades extending across two of the cheek teeth. This dental pattern has long puzzled paleontologists, since it is not directly comparable with the dentition of any other herbivore or carnivore. Not only the strange teeth, but also the short, broad skull, once suggested a specialized plant diet. However, a variety of lines of evidence, including studies of scratches on the tooth surfaces, seem to show that *Thylacoleo* was indeed a carnivore. It used its incisors for stabbing and its blade-tooth for cutting flesh, like the carnassials of creodonts and carnivores (see pages 50 and 66).

Most other Australian marsupial mammals show obvious parallels, or "evolutionary convergences", with placental mammals from other continents. For example, the extinct marsupial "wolf" *Thylacinus* seems to be identical in every respect to a placental dog or fox. The skulls are hard to tell apart, except on close study. One difference is that the molars of *Thylacinus* have both shearing and grinding surfaces, while these two functions are performed by different teeth in the dogs. Similar striking convergences are seen in many other marsupials: there are marsupial moles, marsupial anteaters, marsupial shrews and marsupial leaf-eaters.

The bones of Pleistocene giant marsupials have been found in great numbers in ancient lakes and caves, in various parts of Australia. These date from 50,000 to 12,000 years ago, after which all giant species seem to vanish. It may be that these large animals were vulnerable to human activities, and were hunted to extinction by the earliest aborigines and the dingos they probably brought with them (see chapter six).

Australian marsupials today fall into five main groups, containing 13 families: the opossum-like dasyuroids; the insectivorous bandicoots or perameloids; the kangaroos, and the climbing and gliding marsupials or phalangeriods; the koalas or phascolarctoids; and the wombats or vombatoids.

South America is set free

South America was an island continent for most of the Age of Mammals, from about 75 to 3 million years ago. Marsupials and placentals appear to have spread there

functional one. The other three toes – two, three and five – were much reduced and firmly bound together by connective tissue. No doubt *Procoptodon* moved by hopping, as do modern kangaroos and wallabies. This is a highly efficient method of locomotion and, if anything, slightly less strenuous than running on two or four limbs. Kangaroos can achieve racehorse speeds of 45-55 kilometres per hour (about 30 miles per hour) over short distances.

The ancestry of the kangaroos is not entirely certain. They can be traced back to the Miocene epoch, to small ancestral forms about the size of an opossum. The success of the group is illustrated by the diversity of species that has evolved since, and by their continued abundance today, despite hunting. Indeed, these marsupials can establish themselves almost anywhere, given the chance. Small colonies of wallabies live wild in England, where they have escaped from wildlife parks! Ecologically, kangaroos are the equivalents in Australia of the grazing antelope, deer and cattle in other parts of the world. They may look very different, but they fulfil the same role.

Red kangaroo, Megaleia rufa, *in action. The long tail is an effective counterbalance when kangaroos are moving rapidly. They can bound along almost as fast as a racehorse, and their jumping style of locomotion is just as efficient as the more familiar four-legged galloping of the horse. The red kangaroo is up to 2 metres (almost 7 feet) tall, but much larger kangaroos lived in Australia until relatively recently.*

during the Late Cretaceous, when a land bridge existed for a few million years, as discussed previously. This northern link was broken before the extinction of the dinosaurs, by which time some six or seven mammalian lineages were established. There was still a southern land bridge to Antarctica, and as we have seen, marsupials appear to have crossed over this towards Australia. This bridge was broken by Eocene times, and South American mammals evolved in total isolation thereafter for some 50 million years.

During this time, a spectacular range of endemic (geographically restricted) meat-eating mammals evolved, as strange and unusual as those of Australia. There were marsupial equivalents of sabre-toothed cats, dogs, bears and many others. The herbivores were mainly placental mammals, but not the familiar horses and deer of other regions. There were horse-mimics and hippo-mimics, as well as huge armadillos and sloths, and giant rodents – some as large as deer!

The origins of South American mammals were a mystery until the recent studies of Cretaceous mammals there showed that many typical groups entered from North America, before the Age of Mammals began (see page 101). These included marsupials and South American ungulates, as well as possibly the sloths and armadillos. Other groups, such as bats, monkeys and rodents, appear to have arrived rather later.

The fossil carnivorous marsupial Borhyaena *from the Santa Cruz Formation (Miocene) of Patagonia, Argentina. The dog-like size and features of this animal suggest that it would have been able to hunt herbivores such as small deer.*

Marsupials of the deep south

The marsupials did not undergo such an extensive adaptive radiation in South America as in Australia. This was mainly because placental mammals were present in South America as well, and they took over most of the plant-eating ways of life. Nevertheless marsupials were – and still are – successful as insectivores, carnivores and

PARALLEL EVOLUTION OF SABRE-TOOTHED "CATS"

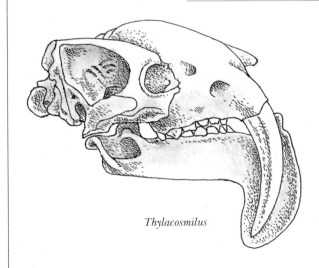

Thylacosmilus

Marsupial and placental mammals are well known for the many examples of parallel evolution. There are marsupial versions of the placental cats, dogs, moles, shrews, squirrels and others. In North America and Europe, biologists tend to view the marsupials as "weak" imitations of the more familiar and local placentals. Yet both evolved at the same time, although entirely independently, and the marsupial sabre-tooth Thylacosmilus *(left) was no doubt just as effective at hunting as the placental sabre-tooth* Smilodon *(right).*

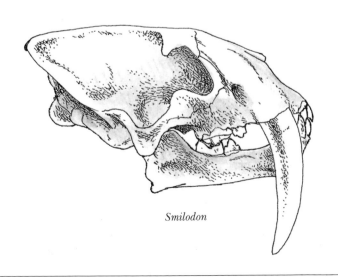

Smilodon

THYLACOSMILUS

This marsupial sabre-toothed carnivore was one of numerous puncture-killers that evolved during the latter part of the Age of Mammals. These animals probably fed on thick-skinned herbivores in all parts of the world, until both predators and prey died out in the last two million years. Thylacosmilus has the longest sabre teeth of any puncture-killer, being 20 centimetres (8 inches) in length. In addition, and uniquely among sabre-tooths, the sabres grew continuously, to compensate for wear at the tips.

small herbivores. There were about ten families in the past, of which three survive today: the didelphid opossums; and the microbiotheres and caenolestids, both mouse-sized insectivores. The herbivorous and carnivorous families have all gone. Most of these showed remarkable evolutionary convergences with placental shrews, cats, sabre-tooths and dogs.

The borhyaenids, such as *Prothylacynus* from the Miocene rocks of Argentina, had short limbs and fairly heavy, dog-like skulls; they ranged in size from a badger to a lion. One poorly preserved specimen seems to indicate a giant borhyaenid with a skull 60 centimetres (24 inches) long! The borhyaenids had plantigrade feet, and were rather bear-like, slow-moving animals, unlike the placental dogs which walk on their toes.

Later relatives of the borhyaenids, the Late Miocene and Pliocene thylacosmilids, are almost indistinguishable from the placental sabre-toothed cats that lived in North America at the same time. The most striking features are the greatly lengthened canine teeth, presumably used for puncturing the hides of thick-skinned South American "notoungulates" (see below). The thylacosmilids such as *Thylacosmilus* itself survived into the Pleistocene, but died out when their large prey disappeared.

Other South American marsupials were smaller animals, such as the insectivorous or omnivorous caenolestids. One representative, *Palaeothentes*, had long lower incisor teeth and blade-like cheek teeth. Another group, the argyrolagids, looked just like modern

(Continued on page 96.)

AUSTRALIA IN THE PLEISTOCENE

One million years ago, on the great grassy plains of southern Australia, the landscape was dominated by marsupials – as it is today, to a lesser extent. In the early to middle Pleistocene, giant versions of many living marsupials wandered freely, including kangaroos and wombats. The giant Pleistocene echidna (lower right), a species of *Zaglossus*, was more than 60 centimetres (two feet) long. The dominant herbivores were the diprotodonts. Three diprotodonts are shown here: *Zygomaturus* with bony protuberances on its snout, hiding behind the tree on the right; *Diprotodon*, a larger creature shown to the left of the tree; and the giant *Palorchestes* to the left of them. Kangaroos are represented by the giant *Procoptodon*. These kangaroos are being harried by a pack of four marsupial "lions", *Thylacoleo*.

The world as it was then.

Most monotremes and marsupials of the Pleistocene epoch in Australia were larger than their modern relatives. This is true of the echidna Zaglossus *(1). The superficially cat-like* Thylacoleo *(2) may have hunted* Zygomaturus *(3),* Procoptodon *(4),* Diprotodon *(5) and* Palorchestes *(6).*

MARSUPIAL EVOLUTION

The fossil record of marsupials is under intensive study, and new finds are being made in Africa, Asia and Antarctica. The diagram shows our evidence so far, for marsupials living in different continents, and suggests how the original members of the group in North America migrated to other regions.

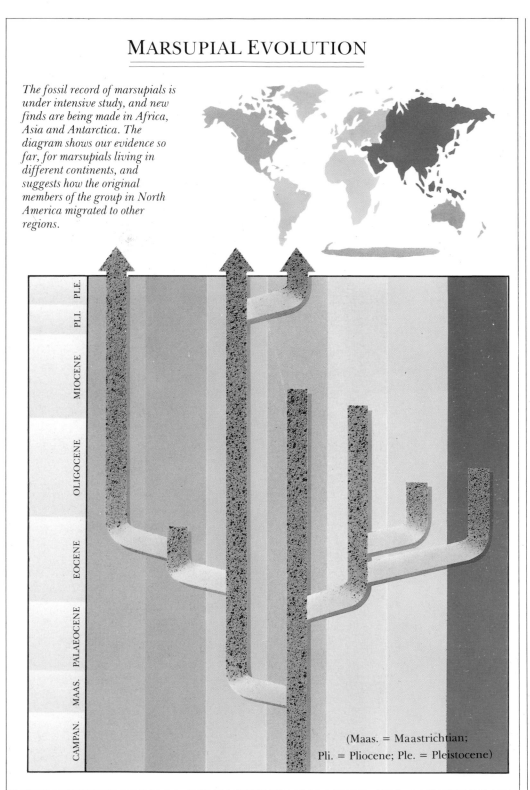

(Maas. = Maastrichtian; Pli. = Pliocene; Ple. = Pleistocene)

kangaroo-rats, with small bodies and extremely long hind limbs adapted for jumping. *Argyrolagus* had a narrow snout and broad cheek teeth for crushing plant material. Several marsupial groups in the Eocene and Oligocene mimicked rodents by having gnawing incisors and tough grinding cheek teeth, but these seem to have given way to true rodents during the Oligocene.

Few teeth, or none at all

Characteristic placental mammals of South America today are the edentates (mammalian order Edentata) such as the sloths and armadillos. These are interesting for a variety of reasons. Ecologically, they have highly specialized lifestyles that are not paralleled closely by other groups elsewhere. In this they differ from the marsupials, which often show similarities with placental mammals. Biogeographically, the distribution of edentates seems to be focused on South America, though they have successfully migrated northwards into Central and North America in the past three million years. However, an anteater has been found in the Eocene Messel deposits of Germany (see page 61). Scientists are still puzzled as to how it got there.

Phylogenetically, the edentates appear to be a separate line of evolution from all other placentals. This implies a fundamental split in the placental branch of evolution during the Late Cretaceous, into edentates – and perhaps pangolins too – and other placentals. The timing of the split is uncertain because the oldest known edentate fossils are Late Palaeocene in age, some 30-40 million years after the supposed date of the division.

The edentates are distinguished from other placentals by extra joints on their vertebrae (backbones), a specialized hip joint, and great reduction in the teeth. Edentates, a term which means "no teeth", may have a few incisors, though the anteaters have none at all. Most have also lost the protective enamel tooth covering. Modern anteaters and armadillos feed on termites, ants and similar insects, which they can swallow without crushing; sloths are herbivorous. In addition, most edentates have long, curved claws which are used either for digging into the nests of ants and termites, or for hanging in the trees, as do sloths.

Fossilized armour

The oldest armadillo fossils are of the armoured scutes (bony plates) characteristic of the group. Even Palaeocene and Eocene versions had bony plates set into the skin of the back and tail, and arranged in rings so that they could flex and overlap when the animal curled up. Most early armadillos resembled the living species, being relatively small. However some were carnivores with sharp teeth, and one had two horn-like bony scutes on its head. But the best-known armadillo fossils belong to an extinct group of giants, the glyptodonts.

The glyptodonts reached enormous sizes in the Pliocene and Pleistocene. *Glyptodon* itself was 1.5 metres (5 feet) high and 3.3 metres (11 feet) long, and it was the most heavily armoured mammal of all time – being reminiscent of a small tank! The plates covered the sides of the body and protected the limbs to some extent. There was a bony skull cap over the top of the head, and bony, spiked rings around the tail. This amazing suit of armour weighed as much as 400 kilograms (900 pounds), one-fifth of the wearer's total weight. It must have been an effective protection against the sabre-toothed thylacosmilids which roamed at that time.

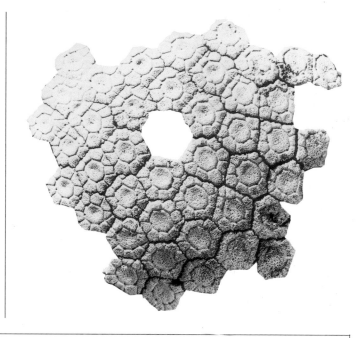

Armour plates of the North American glyptodont Glyptotherium, *from the Pleistocene rocks of the Mexican Gulf. The intricate pattern of interlocking hexagonal plates provided an effective, flexible yet tough armour, that could withstand the sabre-toothed cats, whether marsupial or placental, of the Americas.*

GLYPTODON

The glyptodonts were highly successful plant-eaters that evolved into numerous species in South America, and spread to North America after the joining of the Isthmus of Panama. They owed their success to their superficially turtle-like armour and their powerful claws, which they used for digging up roots and tubers. Glyptodon *might have seemed impregnable, but it and its whole group succumbed only a few tens of thousands of years ago, suffering from a disaster such as catastrophic climatic change, competition from placental mammals – including humans.*

The right foot of the North American *Glyptotherium seen from the top (left) and below (right). The broad, short toes were needed to support the large size of the animal and the weight of its armour.*

Glyptodon's skull was short and deep, as in some of the large Australian marsupials, and the teeth indicate a diet of tough grasses. The broad feet bore long hooves, which may have been used in digging. In some members of the group the tail carried a spiked club that would have been an effective deterrent against interested carnivores!

Slow movers of tree and ground

The tree sloths evolved and diversified from the Eocene epoch onwards. However, as with the armadillos, there was a spectacular yet extinct side branch that is of great interest. These were the ground sloths, some of which, like *Megatherium*, were up to 6 metres (20 feet) long. These animals are usually pictured sitting up on their haunches, feeding on the leaves of tall trees which they pulled down with their long claws.

The biology of ground sloths is known in exceptional detail because they died out only 11,000 years ago, possibly having been hunted to extinction by humans. Extensive remains of bones and even some soft tissues have been collected from caves in South and North America. Some specimens still possess clumps of yellow and red hair, and on these hairs paleontologists have found the remains of powdery green algae that grew there, as happens with modern sloths.

Ground sloth coprolites (fossilized dung) have also been found in vast layers in certain caves, often several metres thick. The dung contains plant fragments and pollen

MEGATHERIUM

The giant ground sloth of South America was another quite recent loss to the world. Indeed, Megatherium has been extinct for only a few thousand years, and preserved samples of its hair and dung are still found. The dung was deposited in vast quantities in caves and other living quarters, and apparently one of these dung deposits in Argentina ignited and burned for six months! Megatherium had a broad bowl-like pelvis, and it squatted like a tripod, balanced on its short hind legs and tail.

The notoungulates were the most successful of all South American herbivores, including more than 100 genera that ranged in size from rabbit to rhino. Fossils of the largest, *Toxodon*, were first collected by Charles Darwin in Argentina. He described it as "perhaps one of the strangest animals ever discovered", since it shared features of the rodents, rhino and manatees. Another unusual feature of *Toxodon*, which it shared with most of the South American forms, is that its teeth continued to grow throughout life, and were thus able to keep up with wear produced by grinding tough food.

Astrapotherium was as large as a rhino, and had a long body with short legs. The high nostrils suggest that it too

which show seasonal and long-term variations in the diet. At times the giant sloths fed on desert plants such as creosote bush, yucca, snakeweed and cactus; when climates were cooler and wetter they turned to sagebrush, pine, birch and juniper. Desert plants are not eaten significantly by herbivorous mammals today, so the giant ground sloths successfully exploited a unique source of food and their ecological niche has not been filled since their extinction.

Anteaters have a poorer fossil record than armadillos and sloths, consisting of only two or three species from the Miocene and Pliocene. They were broadly like living species. The oddest quirk of their history is that the oldest anteater is *Eurotamandua*, from the Eocene of Germany (see page 61).

Ungulate imposters

For most of the Tertiary period, the main plant-eaters in South America were placental mammals that looked similar to ungulates such as horses, camels, deer and rhinos. However, they were in fact members of two groups – litopterns and notoungulates – that were unique to South America, and which may not be closely related to the more familiar ungulate groups elsewhere.

The litopterns looked like rabbits, horses and camels and filled similar ecological roles, but the details of their skeletons differ from true ungulates. *Diadiaphorus* from the Miocene and Pliocene was a lightly-built animal which looked remarkably like a horse, having long limbs and a single central hoof touching the ground. *Macrauchenia* had a lengthy neck, like a camel, and broad rhino-type feet. Its fossils show that its nostrils were placed high on the skull, which suggests that it had an elephant-like trunk.

MACRAUCHENIA

One of the oddest South American ungulates, Macrauchenia, *was rather camel-like in proportions – except for its short, flexible trunk. There is little doubt about the trunk since* Macrauchenia, *like other South American ungulates, had a centrally-placed nostril high on its head, almost between the eyes, exactly as in today's elephants. The trunk may have gathered leaves from tall trees.*

had a trunk, which it may have used together with long, forwards-pointing incisor teeth for digging up water plants and roots. Other notoungulates included the pyrotheres, also long-bodied animals with trunks. They seem to parallel elephants, in their skeleton and in the tusk-like incisor teeth set firmly in the skull.

South American waifs

Several small-scale invasions of the South American island continent may have taken place in the Oligocene and Miocene, when odd stragglers from a variety of placental groups arrived. Perhaps they island-hopped across the Caribbean, or floated on small rafts of matted plants, or flew there. These waifs include bats, monkeys and rodents, all of which arrived well after the establishment of the more typical mammals already described – but well before the opening of the land bridge to Central America, three million years ago.

The rodents are of particular interest, since several groups became highly successful in South America. These are typified today by the guinea pig and its relatives, the largest of which is the capybara, weighing in at a hefty 50 kilograms (110 pounds). However, extinct relatives were as large as bears or even small rhinos: the dinomyids, a

A front view of the head and forequarters of the elephant-like Toxodon, *from Pleistocene times in Argentina. The broad, spatula-shaped snout, lined with blunt incisor teeth, was presumably used to gather waterside plants or sift through mud. With its heavy skeleton and massive shoulders, like the rhino,* Toxodon *reached an overall body length of 2.7 metres (nine feet).*

THE GREAT AMERICAN INTERCHANGE

The mammals of South America evolved in isolation for most of the Tertiary period. Certain groups, such as bats, managed to "travel-hop" across the Caribbean islands, or from Africa, but the continent was largely cut off from other major land masses by about 60 million years ago. Then, only three million years ago, the Isthmus of Panama rose from the sea, and South America joined Central and North America. A flood of mammals moved northwards from the south, and also southwards from Central and North America.

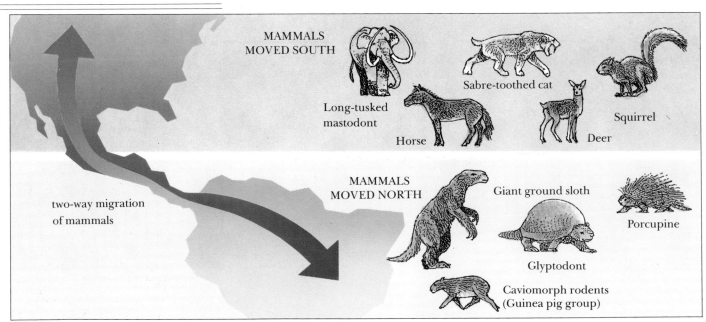

name which means "terrible mice", include *Telicomys* from the Late Miocene and Pliocene of Argentina, which stood about one metre (three feet) in height. These unusual animals were ecological equivalents of deer and goats, rather than mice and hamsters.

The great American interchange

Three million years ago, during the Pliocene, life in South America was disrupted by the formation of a land bridge across to the southern tip of Central America. This enabled a whole range of North American mammals such as racoons, rabbits, dogs, horses, deer, camels, bears, pumas and mastodont elephants to head south; it also allowed South American opossums, armadillos, glyptodonts, ground sloths, anteaters, monkeys and porcupines to move north.

The standard interpretation of this event has been that the "superior" northern invaders defeated the South American mammals, and drove most of them to extinction. However, detailed studies have now shown that the situation was not so simple.

Firstly, the size of the two invasions was actually balanced at the levels of families, and the extinction rate at the level of genera. About 15 families invaded from north

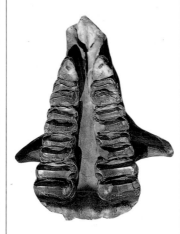

The palate (roof of the mouth) of the pyrothere Pyrotherium romeri, *from the Miocene-aged Deseado Formation of Argentina. This part of the 85-centimetre (34-inch) skull shows the many broad grinding cheek teeth.*

to south, and 15 from south to north. At the level of genera, the invasions led to 13 per cent extinction in South America and 11 per cent extinction in North America. However, the numbers of genera that invaded were not the same – many more moved into South America than spread north. How could the numbers of genera invading be so different, and yet extinction levels be roughly the same? The North American invaders did not generally cause South American forms to die off; they "insinuated" themselves into the wildlife, finding unoccupied ecological roles and niches, and actually increased the overall diversity of mammals in South America. Before the invasion, there were 72 mammal genera in South America, compared to 170 today; in North America the total increased from 131 to only 141 today. There seem to have been fewer opportunities to insinuate in the north!

The second error that has been made in the past, has been to assume that most of the South American mammals which became extinct did so as a result of competition from their northern invaders. However, the extinctions were already in train for some of these groups, such as the notoungulates and litopterns. Other groups died out long after the invasion, and at the same time as many of the northern invaders disappeared themselves. The causes of these Late Pleistocene extinctions were not related to the "Great American Interchange" more than two million years earlier (see chapter six).

Finally, the sums have to be applied to the correct land masses. It has been common to compare South America to North America. However, the land bridge was at the southern extent of Central America, and so Central America must be considered on the North American side. It is true that many South American forms, such as monkeys, giant rodents, tree sloths, anteaters and toxodonts, never entered North America – but they were successful enough in Central America.

Sadly, most of these fascinating South American mammals have now disappeared. There are no more giant ground sloths and glyptodonts, no more litopterns or notoungulates, no more thylacosmilids or borhyaenids. The causes of these extinctions are just as mysterious as those of the diprotodonts and giant kangaroos in Australia, and of the mammoths and woolly rhinos in northern parts of the world (see chapter six). These extinctions may even be connected globally, forging a link between the mammals of South America and Australia that had not occurred since the beginning of the Cretaceous period.

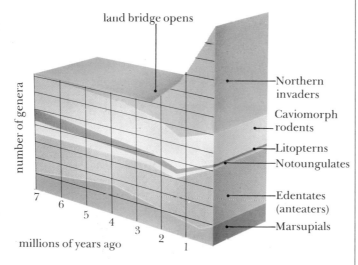

The traditional view of the Great American Interchange has been that the "invaders" from the north were superior to the mammals of South America, and drove them to extinction. However, this was not the case, as the diagram (right) shows. South America suffered very modest losses, and most of the northerners managed to fit in, without causing extinctions. The unusual South American mammals died out some two million years or more later, in the Late Pleistocene – as a result of climatic changes, or perhaps human interference.

land bridge opens

number of genera

Northern invaders

Caviomorph rodents

Litopterns

Notoungulates

Edentates (anteaters)

Marsupials

7 6 5 4 3 2 1

millions of years ago

CHAPTER FIVE

THE AGE OF THE UNGULATES

The high point in the evolution of many mammalian groups from North America and Europe, occurred during the Miocene and Pliocene epochs, 24-2 million years ago. The horses, rhinoceroses and their unusual relatives were diverse and successful on several continents. Camels and pigs were abundant in North America, while the horned ruminants, such as deer and cattle, were diversifying widely in northern parts of the world, as well as in Africa and Asia. The elephants were enjoying great success worldwide, which may be hard to believe from their present rather depleted numbers. All of these grazing and browsing herbivores are commonly called ungulates, meaning "hoofed".

Other groups were no less successful during these times: gnawing rodents, large carnivores that preyed on the thick-skinned plant-eaters, and even our own line, the primates, were blossoming.

These bursts of evolutionary success occurred in a world in which conditions were changing rapidly from those of the earlier part of the Tertiary period (see chapters two and three). Climates were becoming cooler worldwide, although average temperatures were still some 5-6°C warmer than today. This fall in temperature was occasioned by continental movements and the development of an ice cap at the South Pole. During both the Age of Dinosaurs and the Age of Mammals, the continents had been drifting apart from their former fusion as the great supercontinent of Pangaea (see page 86).

By Miocene times, the distribution of continents was approaching its modern configuration, although the Atlan-

The giant Miocene beaver Palaeocastor fossor *from rocks of the Harrison Beds, Sioux County, Nebraska, USA (opposite). This photograph shows the front half of the body, and especially the powerful front limbs with their broad hands. The lower jaws have been split and placed on either side of the skull.* Palaeocastor, *unlike modern beavers, did not build dams, but it did dig complex, deep and spiralling burrows.*

tic Ocean was narrower and South America was still an island. Nevertheless Antarctica drifted southwards until part of it lay over the South Pole, and this triggered the development of an ice cap. So long as the Poles were covered by ocean, an ice cap did not form, since the sea water allows mixing and transport of heat to the polar regions. However, continents become colder away from coastal areas, and the larger they are, the colder they get. Once winter ice began to collect on Antarctica as it moved to the South Pole, the white surface of the ice reflected sunlight, and contributed to the cooling effect – and to its own growth.

The vast grasslands

While the growth of an ice sheet at the South Pole obviously had profound effects on any mammals that lived on Antarctica, the main global effect was the spread of grasslands. Cooler, drier climates meant that the lush tropical and subtropical forests diminished in size. Northern and southern continents – North America and Europe, Africa and South America – acquired a new kind of landscape, with vast expanses of dry grassland: prairies, steppes, savannahs and pampas, respectively.

Grasses are members of a large group of flowering plants that are adapted to cover huge areas of dry lowland, and to withstand heavy grazing. They contain large amounts of silica, the same chemical as sand, which prevents soft-toothed animals from eating them, and has forced many ungulate groups to develop tougher teeth. Grasses also have tenacious roots and breeding structures very low down, so that they can survive and seed even when cropped close to the ground. Grasses had come on the scene before the

Miocene, but it was only then that they came to dominate many parts of the world.

In many respects, it is true to say that the ungulates created the grasslands. Close cropping of plants by herbivorous mammals actually improves the survival chances of grasses compared to other plants, and this can be observed today. At the edges of forests, there may be a mixed flora of low shrubs, small seedlings from the trees and shrubs, various broad-leaved flowering plants, and some grasses. Heavy grazing mows everything down to ground level, and this kills off the seedlings of trees and bushes, and most of the broad-leaved plants. Only the grasses survive. Hence in Late Oligocene and Early Miocene times, some 30-20 million years ago, the early horses, rhinos and deer were probably carving out the embryonic prairies that we see today.

The horse Neohipparion *(below) was one of numerous horses that lived in North America during the Miocene period. This animal was relatively advanced for its time, and differs from modern horses only in small details: it was smaller, and there were still three toes on each foot, even if the two side toes did not reach the ground.*

The need to be tall and fleet

The large grasslands changed the course of mammalian evolution by stimulating a great adaptive radiation of various ungulate groups, and indeed it may have been a precursor to the evolution of humans. Grasslands support a greater density of large animals than can a mixed forest. The range of feeding types increases, with specialized grazers that feed on different levels of grass. For example, horses eat rather roughly and indiscriminately, while sheep nip off the leftover clumps of grass right to the roots. There is also space for browsers that feed on leaves of occasional bushes and trees, and for smaller animals that feed on grass seeds.

The nature of the grasses, their hardness and indigestibility, led to major changes in the teeth and digestive tracts of most ungulates, especially in the ruminants (see

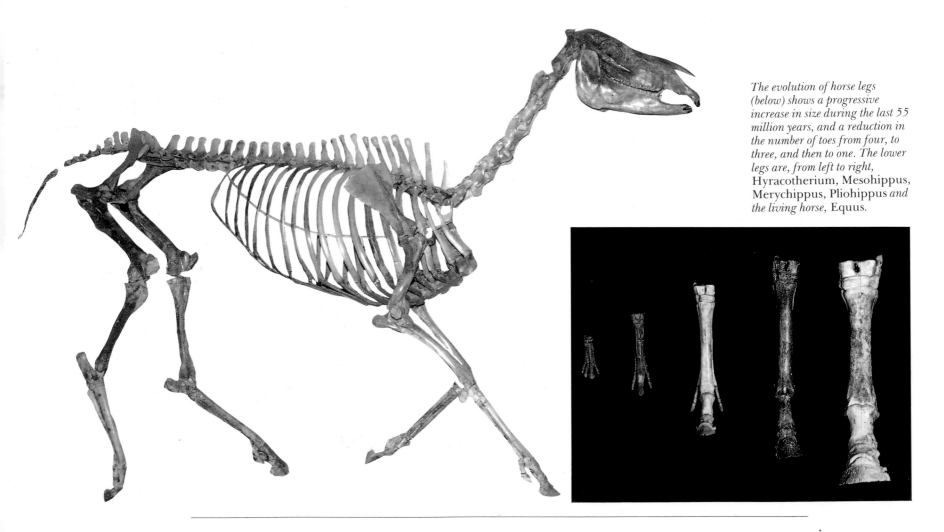

The evolution of horse legs (below) shows a progressive increase in size during the last 55 million years, and a reduction in the number of toes from four, to three, and then to one. The lower legs are, from left to right, Hyracotherium, Mesohippus, Merychippus, Pliohippus *and the living horse,* Equus.

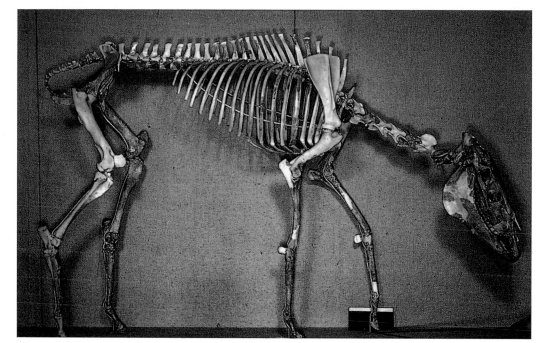

A fossil skeleton of Pliohippus *(right), a North American horse that was very similar to the modern species. This was the first truly one-toed horse, and it spread across North America in the Late Miocene, replacing the previous versions such as* Merychippus *and* Hipparion.

The skull of Equus, *today's horse (below). This very young or "subrecent" fossil shows the massively tall lower jaw designed to accommodate the straight battery of deeply-rooted, continuously-growing cheek teeth, and also to provide a broad attachment area for the powerful chewing muscles.*

page 108). The grasslands also occasioned major changes in the skeletons of various animals. Herbivores could no longer rely on camouflage and small size to escape predation. They had to become tall to see their enemies, and fleet of foot to escape them. This is why there was a great change in the evolution of ungulate limbs and overall body sizes during the Miocene. The same pressures probably caused certain early tree-living African apes to become upright and bipedal during the Late Miocene – the beginnings of the human line.

Textbook evolution?

The horses, rhinos, and tapirs of the order Perissodactyla, had enjoyed great success in the Eocene and Oligocene – both as modest-sized forest browsers (horses and tapirs) and as small-to-large open-habitat herbivores (rhinos and brontotheres, see page 76).

Horse evolution was stimulated in another direction by the spread of grasslands, and this story has become one of the classic cases of evolution that is reproduced endlessly in textbooks. Several major changes took place in the horses, in particular during the Oligocene and Miocene. They became larger, increasing from the terrier size of their early history to the sizeable creature that is the modern horse. Their limbs became longer and more slender, the number of toes was reduced from three or

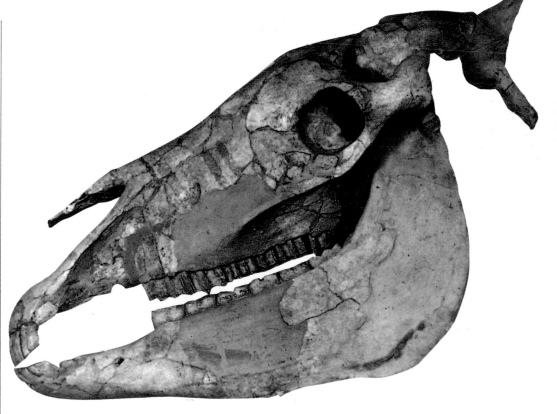

four on each foot to a single functional middle toe with a large hoof, and the teeth became more deeply rooted and grew continuously.

These changes exemplify responses to a shift of habitat, from forest to open prairie. Large size, long limbs and the single hoof are adaptations for seeing enemies better and escaping from them faster. It is no wonder that horses today are successful in racing – for that is what they evolved to do, on the Miocene grasslands.

The deeper, continuously-growing cheek teeth are also a response to a shift, this time in diet, from soft leaves to hard, silica-rich grasses. Indeed, the wear and tear of grazing is so great that modern horses have teeth that are five or six times as deep as they are broad, quite different from the teeth of their ancestors. This immense depth, and the need for powerful jaw muscles, has changed the whole shape of the skull.

The story of horse evolution is a textbook case since there is apparently a single line of evolution, with a succession of ever-changing forms popping up every few million years: *Hyracotherium* ("Eohippus") in the Eocene, *Mesohippus* in the Oligocene, *Parahippus* and *Merychippus* in the Miocene, *Pliohippus* in the Pliocene, and *Equus* in the Pleistocene and today. We can discern a neat sequence of changes in the teeth, skull, brain, limbs and overall body size.

However, the evolution of horses did not in fact follow such a simple path. True, these broad changes did take place in the order described, but there were many side branches and other forms of horses that complicate the pattern.

Horses of the prairies

The main lineages of horses evolved in North America, as far as we can tell. Periodically they sent out side branches to other parts of the world. There were four separate horse migrations into Europe and Asia in the Eocene, Miocene, Pliocene and Pleistocene, and two into South America, in the Pliocene and Pleistocene. But it is ironic that horses have now died out in the wild in the continent of their greatest past success.

One of the most successful horses was *Hipparion*, which originated in Middle Miocene times in North America. It invaded Europe, Asia and Africa in several waves during the Late Miocene, Pliocene and Pleistocene. This highly successful horse was a side branch, however, and not related to modern horses, hence it is usually omitted from the simplified evolutionary trees! Overall, dozens of

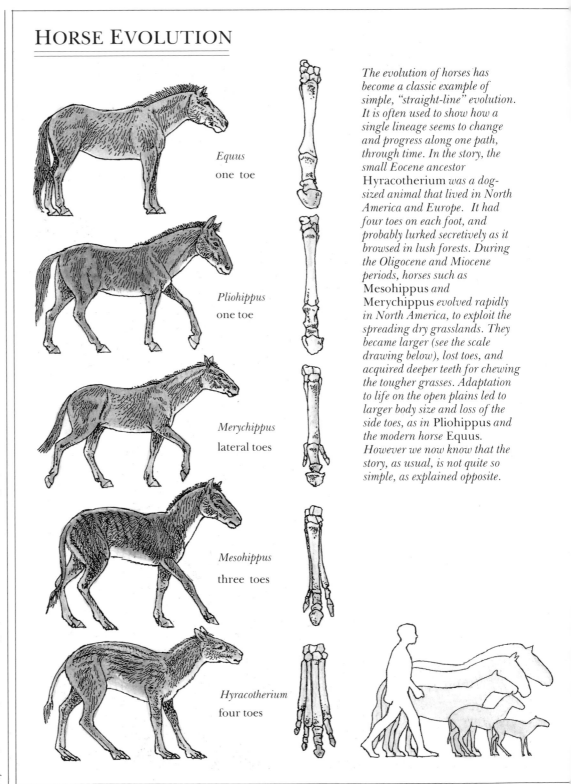

HORSE EVOLUTION

Equus
one toe

Pliohippus
one toe

Merychippus
lateral toes

Mesohippus
three toes

Hyracotherium
four toes

The evolution of horses has become a classic example of simple, "straight-line" evolution. It is often used to show how a single lineage seems to change and progress along one path, through time. In the story, the small Eocene ancestor Hyracotherium *was a dog-sized animal that lived in North America and Europe. It had four toes on each foot, and probably lurked secretively as it browsed in lush forests. During the Oligocene and Miocene periods, horses such as* Mesohippus *and* Merychippus *evolved rapidly in North America, to exploit the spreading dry grasslands. They became larger (see the scale drawing below), lost toes, and acquired deeper teeth for chewing the tougher grasses. Adaptation to life on the open plains led to larger body size and loss of the side toes, as in* Pliohippus *and the modern horse* Equus. *However we now know that the story, as usual, is not quite so simple, as explained opposite.*

species of horses evolved, and as many as six may have lived side by side on the North American prairies in Miocene times.

Tapirs and rhinos, relatives of the horses, continued to evolve through the Miocene and Pliocene, but they were not so significant as the horses. Indeed the rhinos had already passed the climax of their evolution, which occurred in the Oligocene (see page 76). During the Miocene, the rhinos crossed to Africa, and later to Asia, where they survive today.

The extinct chalicotheres, relatives of the brontotheres (see page 76), were important animals in the landscapes of the Miocene and Pliocene epochs of North America, Europe and Asia. They survived in Africa until the Pleistocene. *Chalicotherium* from the Miocene of Eurasia and Africa was arguably the most unusual mammal of all time: it looked like a cross between a horse and a gorilla! The head was roughly horse-shaped, but the fore limbs were very long and the hind limbs short. The pelvis was low and broad, as in the unrelated ground sloths (see page 98), and it is likely that *Chalicotherium* sat on its haunches to feed on leaves from low trees. The fingers of the hand bore small hooves, and the toes had small claws which may have been used for digging up roots. It seems that *Chalicotherium* walked with its hands curled up, an unusual parallel with the knuckle-walking of gorillas and chimps. The chalicotheres may seem strange animals to include in the perissodactyl group, but they showed all the right characters, and they even shared a few specialized features with the brontotheres.

Advantages of the pacing gait

The even-toed ungulates (artiodactyls) had a long and successful history before the Miocene (see page 77), but their fortunes improved even further with the spread of the grasslands and the evolution of new ways to cope with the fresh opportunities. The oreodonts and some other artiodactyl groups passed from the Oligocene into the Early Miocene, but only the pigs and hippos survive to the present day. Camels and ruminants were also present as relatively minor groups in the Oligocene, but they were to evolve dramatically from the Miocene onwards, particularly the ruminants.

Most of camel evolution took place in North America although, oddly, the group is no longer represented there. Oligocene camels probably looked rather goat-like (see page 78), but Miocene versions became much modified as a result of the spread of grasslands. They increased in

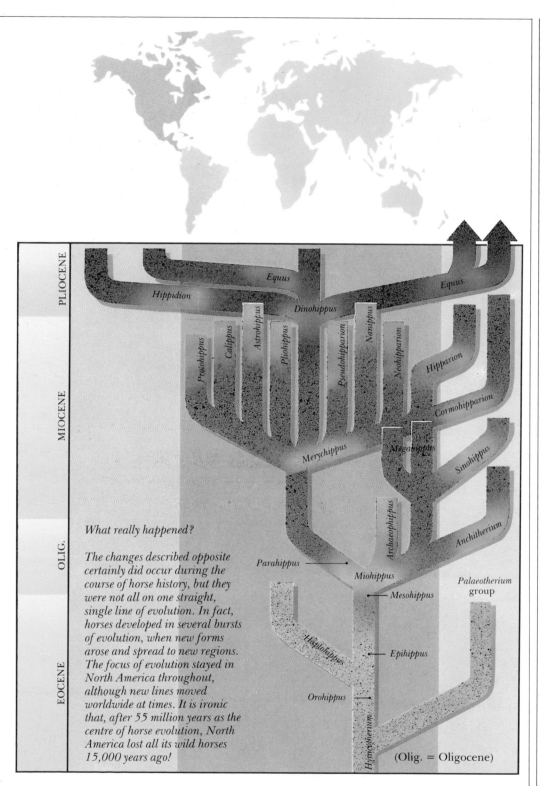

What really happened?

The changes described opposite certainly did occur during the course of horse history, but they were not all on one straight, single line of evolution. In fact, horses developed in several bursts of evolution, when new forms arose and spread to new regions. The focus of evolution stayed in North America throughout, although new lines moved worldwide at times. It is ironic that, after 55 million years as the centre of horse evolution, North America lost all its wild horses 15,000 years ago!

(Olig. = Oligocene)

CHALICOTHERIUM

This looks like an imaginary mammal composed of the rear parts of a ground sloth, the arms of a gorilla and a horse's head. But it was real enough, as shown by numerous complete fossil skeletons from the Miocene period of Europe and Africa, and also by relatives from North America and Asia. Perhaps Chalicotherium could stand on two legs when necessary, rearing up on its back limbs to a height of four metres (13 feet), to eat foliage from trees.

size, and their necks and limbs became longer. By Mid Miocene times, they seem to have evolved their peculiar "pacing gait", in which both legs on the right side take one stride, followed by both legs on the left side. This is a highly efficient way of traversing open prairies, and fossilized tracks are evidence that this method of locomotion was used in the Miocene. Further stages in camel evolution at this time were the development of broad pads on the feet, an adaptation for crossing soft earth and sand, and a bony pad to replace the two front upper incisor teeth. Some Miocene camels were antelope-shaped, while one lineage, the giraffe-camels such as

Alticamelus, achieved heights of 3 metres (10 feet) or more, of which nearly half was a greatly elongated neck. In the Pliocene, the camel group invaded South America – where they survive today as the llamas – as well as North Africa and the Middle East, their present home.

Chewing the cud

The main group of selenodont artiodactyls, those with "moon"-shaped cusps on their teeth, are the ruminants. These familiar animals – cattle, sheep, antelopes and deer – are the most abundant and successful ungulates alive today. Their success is relatively recent, and they appear

to owe it to their prodigious digestive systems.

Ruminants are so called because they ruminate, or regurgitate their food as a normal part of digestion. The cow has a four-chambered stomach. A mouthful of grass enters the first chamber, the rumen, where it is broken down to some extent by "friendly" bacteria living there. The food is later brought back up into the mouth for rumination, or "chewing the cud", before passing through the other three stomach chambers, the abomasum, omasum and reticulum, where it is further digested. This arrangement allows a cow to extract the maximum nutritive value from its food, which takes about 80 hours to pass through the system.

Camels also have a ruminating system, but other plant-eaters such as pigs, rhinos and horses lack it, and pass their food within 48 hours. They cannot extract so much nourishment from poor grass as can a ruminant, although they can eat more rapidly. One way to assess the ruminating and non-ruminating systems is to compare the droppings of a cow and a horse. The former is near-liquid, while the latter is more solid.

The first ruminants appeared in the Late Eocene. Their fossils have to be recognized by characters of the ankle and teeth, not by the nature of their stomachs, which do not fossilize! Ruminants have also reduced or lost their upper incisors and have only a horny pad, against which the lower incisors nip off pieces of food, as in the camels. An early ruminant was *Hypertragulus* from the Oligocene of North America. It was a rabbit-sized animal that looked little different from many of the other contemporary artiodactyls (see page 77), but it had the ruminant horny mouth pad.

The extraordinarily long skull of the Miocene camel Floridatragulus *without its lower jaw (above). The eye socket is near the back, with the cheek teeth just in front. The purpose of the extremely long snout, largely toothless except for one or two incisors at the front, is still a mystery.*

A fossil skeleton of the chalicothere Moropus cooki, *from Early Miocene rocks in Wyoming, USA. The skull was remarkably horse-like, yet the broad, powerful hands and feet were quite unlike the slim running limbs of the horses; they were probably adapted for digging.*

The skull of the unusual horned dromomerycid Sinclairomeryx, *which lived in Miocene times in North America. The strange curved horns are quite different from the horns of deer and cattle: they grow out of the frontal bones, just above and behind the eye sockets. These "horns" are equivalent to those of giraffes, only larger, and in life they were covered by skin. The dromomerycids are regarded by some as ancestral to various living groups such as giraffes, deer and cattle.*

Horns and antlers

The ruminants do not seem to have contributed significantly to fossil mammal finds until the Middle and Late Miocene, when the modern groups appear. The evolutionary radiation was triggered, once again, by the great spread of grasslands. Ruminant lines were the tragulids ("mouse deer"), deer, giraffes, cattle and antelopes.

Nearly all ruminants have horns or antlers of some kind. In cattle and sheep, the horn is a bony core surrounded by a permanent horny sheath; in deer, the antler is a bony structure that is shed annually; while in giraffes, the horns are permanent bony structures covered by skin. It seems likely that each kind of horn or antler evolved independently in each major group, as a fighting and display structure. Ruminant males use their horns in head-butting (sheep), "antler wrestling" (deer), or display and threat (cattle. antelope). These activities are involved in establishing social dominance and rank within a herd, winning females, and defending feeding territories. Plant-eaters such as horses and camels do not have horns or antlers, since they live in more open grasslands and eat less food which is less clumped in its distribution, so that territories are unnecessary.

The horns and antlers of ruminants have evolved in a wide variety of shapes and sizes, and fossil species increase that diversity. An antler span of 3.5 metres (11½ feet) has been measured in the extinct Irish deer *Megaloceros*, and even 4 metres (more than 13 feet) in some extinct cattle. The horns may be placed on the forehead or, more rarely, farther forwards. They may be straight, spiralling or branched, and either circular or flat in cross-section.

The greatest bursts of evolution of these advanced ruminants took place in the Late Miocene, Pliocene and Pleistocene epochs, in North America and Eurasia.

Giraffes date back to the Early and Middle Miocene of Europe and Africa. *Samotherium*, from the Late Miocene of Eurasia and Africa, was a typical early form, with short blunt horns on top of its head, and a short neck. *Sivatherium*, from Pleistocene rocks of Africa and Asia, was a heavily-built animal that looked more like a moose than a giraffe. It had a pair of broad "antlers", and stood 2.5 metres (8 feet) tall.

Deer arose in the Middle Miocene in Europe. They soon spread worldwide, with rapid evolution of antlers into a great range of sizes and types. The bovids, including cattle, sheep, goats and antelopes, also appeared in the Middle Miocene, and they have shown the most spectacular evolution of all during the past 15 million years. By Late Miocene times there were 70 genera, increasing to 100 by the Pleistocene, although there are now only about 50. It is remarkable to realize that the divergence between living species such as sheep, bison and oryx has taken place in only a few million years!

These explosive evolutionary radiations could have been triggered solely by the great success of ruminants on

The pronghorn Cosoryx *from the North American Miocene period (right). The pronghorns, or antilocaprids, were once a diverse group of 40 genera, but only one species survives – the pronghorn antelope,* Antilocapra. Cosoryx *is noted for the large, catapult-shaped horns over its eye sockets.*

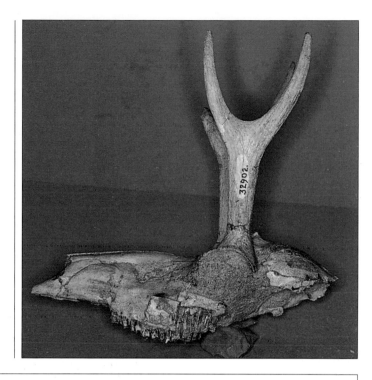

HORNS AND ANTLERS

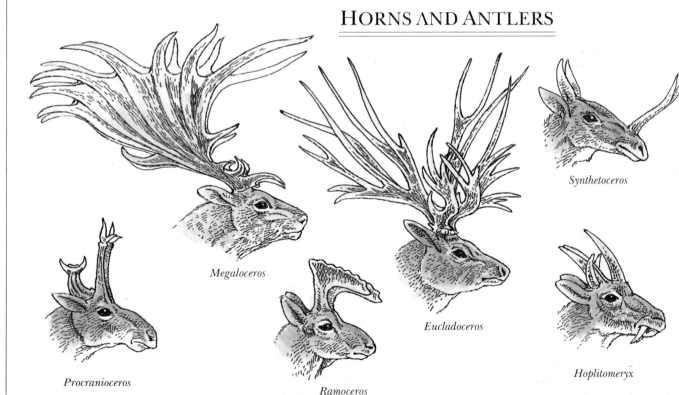

Megaloceros

Procranioceros

Ramoceros

Eucladoceros

Synthetoceros

Hoplitomeryx

Today, the most successful ungulates – that is, large herbivorous mammals – are the horned, even-toed artiodactyls, such as deer, antelope, cattle and giraffes. The term "horn" includes a great range of shapes and types, and it is almost certain that horns evolved independently four or five times. Only cattle and antelope have true horns, consisting of a bony core and a horny sheath, neither of which are shed. Giraffes have the bony core covered with skin, while deer have antlers which are shed annually. These creatures are all deer except for Ramoceros, *which is a pronghorn, and* Synthetoceros, *which is a protoceratid (an extinct horned group).*

the new grasslands. However, many paleontologists have assumed that there were also links with the demise of the perissodactyls, the horses and rhinos. Formerly so successful, these appear to have declined from Early Miocene times. Did the artiodactyls win out over the perissodactyls on those early prairies and steppes?

The battle of the toes: odd versus even

There is no doubt that the Oligocene savannahs and forests of North America and Asia were dominated by perissodactyls (odd-toes) such as early horses, rhinos, brontotheres and chalicotheres. The artiodactyls (even-toes) including camels, pigs and ruminants rose to prominence after the Middle Miocene. Today, there are 79 genera of artiodactyls, but only six of perissodactyls.

The story of how this changeover happened is often quoted as a classic example of competitive replacement, when one group is forced out by another that is evolutionarily much superior, or that is favoured by the changing environment. The omnivorous pigs and their relatives,

and the ruminating camels and cattle, were able to sweep away all opposition on the vast grasslands of the major continents. The perissodactyls are pictured as having flourished in the Eocene and Oligocene, but then they went into a decline that has continued ever since, as a result of the burgeoning success of the artiodactyls.

However, the facts do not support this view. The trends in the diversity of perissodactyls and artiodactyls, at the level of genera and families, have been plotted for the entire history of both groups. There is no evidence for a decline of the former matched by a rise of the latter. In fact, both groups followed similar paths: when one declined in diversity, so did the other; when one increased, so too did the other. These parallel paths of diversification and decline suggest that the two groups were relatively independent, but responding in a similar way to changes in the environment. The relatively recent success of the artiodactyls has happened for a variety of reasons, but in itself it did not cause the perissodactyls to decline.

The horns of Rakomeryx, *a dromomerycid related to* Sinclairomeryx *(see page 110). This is a portion of the skull roof, broken off just above the eye sockets.*

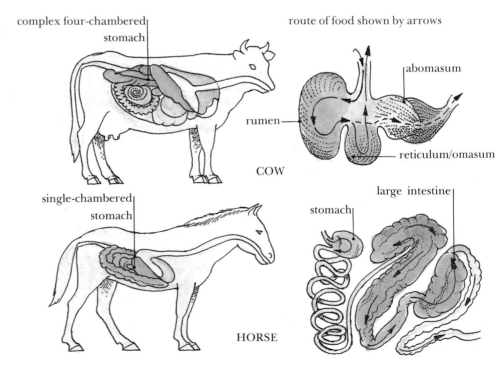

WHO CHEWS THE CUD?

complex four-chambered stomach

route of food shown by arrows

abomasum

rumen

reticulum/omasum

COW

single-chambered stomach

large intestine

stomach

HORSE

A further problem with the competition argument has been the assertion that the artiodactyl digestive system (particularly in the ruminants) is superior to that of perissodactyls. However, detailed comparisons of their workings have shown that one system is not better or worse than the other, simply different. In some conditions ruminants have the edge, while other situations favour perissodactyls. Ruminants can certainly extract more nutrients from a given quantity of food, but perissodactyls are better adapted to cope with highly fibrous fodder.

The coming of the elephants

Today there are only two species of elephant, African and Asian. They are a sorry remnant of the former glory of the mammalian order Proboscidea. More than 30 proboscidean genera are known from fossils, most being Miocene in age.

The early evolution of the group took place mainly in Africa. The oldest elephant remains, from Early Eocene rocks in Algeria, are from an animal one metre (three feet)

A lower jaw of the Miocene elephant Deinotherium *being excavated in Africa (right). The cheek teeth are in the middle of the picture, facing right, and the lower jaws bend away to the left. This down-curved portion bore short tusks in life, although they appear to be missing in this specimen.*

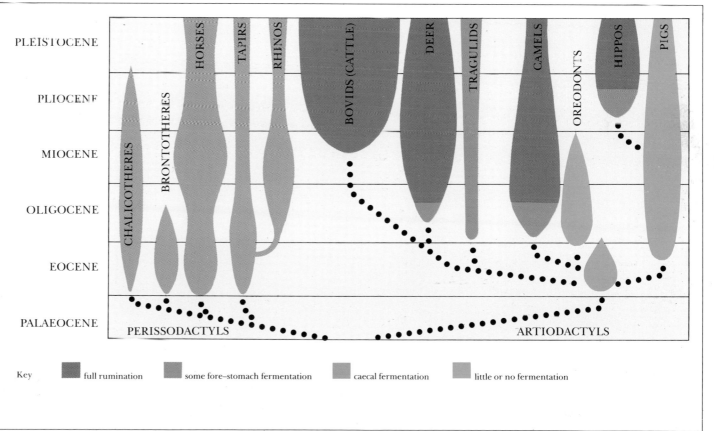

The ruminants – cattle, deer, camels – have a unique digestive system in which food passes through a complex multi-chambered stomach, to be digested in several phases over a long period. After swallowing, the food goes first into the rumen. It is regurgitated for further chewing in the mouth (chewing the cud), then passes through the reticulum, omasum and abomasum, which are three more specialized stomach chambers that further break down and ferment the grass. Horses have a typical non-ruminant digestive system, as is also present in all other mammals. The grass goes straight to the stomach where it is digested as far as possible, and then it passes into the intestine, without any secondary digestion or fermentation. Rumination evolved several times in ungulate history (as shown by the evolutionary tree, right), and there seem to be grades of fermenting activity in the various groups.

PLEISTOCENE
PLIOCENE
MIOCENE
OLIGOCENE
EOCENE
PALAEOCENE

CHALICOTHERES
BRONTOTHERES
HORSES
TAPIRS
RHINOS
BOVIDS (CATTLE)
DEER
TRAGULIDS
CAMELS
OREODONTS
HIPPOS
PIGS

PERISSODACTYLS
ARTIODACTYLS

Key   full rumination   some fore–stomach fermentation   caecal fermentation   little or no fermentation

tall, with a deep skull, a short trunk, and pillar-like legs. *Moeritherium*, from the Late Eocene and Oligocene of North Africa, also had a deep skull, and two of its upper incisor teeth were modified into short tusks. It seems likely that these early forms lived in fresh waters, feeding on aquatic plants in the manner of small hippos.

Several lines of elephant evolution diverged from these ancestral forms in the Oligocene and Miocene. The trends were to larger size, fewer teeth and a trunk. These elephants achieved heights of about 3.5 metres (11 feet) at the shoulder, and the changes in the teeth and trunk appear to be associated with the increase in body size.

Elephants have tusks for defence and gathering food. Larger size, and the presence of tusks, meant that the head became very heavy. (The head of a modern elephant may weigh one tonne!) This vast head had to be supported by a short neck and powerful muscles, which meant that the creature could not reach the ground with its mouth. Hence the flexible, lightweight trunk, which can pick up food and other objects and transfer them to the mouth, like a sensitive feeding arm.

Modern elephants have only one cheek tooth in action

The preserved skeleton of a four-tusked elephant, Gomphotherium, *from the Miocene sediments of Europe and Africa (above). It had two long tusks in the upper jaws, as in modern elephants, but these were straight instead of curved, and supplemented by a pair of straight tusks in the lower jaws. The four tusks appeared to interlock, but their function is uncertain; perhaps they were used with the trunk, to gather up bundles of vegetation and pass them into the mouth.*

The skull of Moeritherium *(right), the most completely known early proboscidean, and ancestral to later elephants. Numerous skeletons have been recovered from the Eocene rocks of Egypt, and in life it was* probably more like a pygmy hippo than an elephant. The jaws had five or six square cheek teeth, as seen here – a primitive feature, since later elephants show a reduction in the number of molars in use at any one time.*

in each side of each jaw, giving a total of four teeth at any one time. This seems to relate to their size and longevity. Because of their bulk, modern elephants have long lives – up to 75 years – and this leads to problems of tooth wear. An elephant eating abrasive plant material has the problem of keeping its teeth in efficient operation for such a long time. Early elephants had all six cheek teeth in each side of each jaw at the same time, the standard mammalian pattern. Modern elephants still have all these teeth, but they come into action one after the other, in sequence. At any one time one tooth is being used, and the others are lined up behind in an embryonic state while older, worn ones fall out. The teeth move forward relative to the jaw as the animal grows. Molars onc to three are in use while the elephant is young, number four comes in at age 4-5 years, number five at 12-13 years, and number

six at age 25 or so. This final tooth has an awesome task, since it must see the elephant through the rest of its life. When tooth six has been worn down, the elephant starves and dies.

One proboscidean line, the deinotheres, lived until the end of the Pliocene in the Old World. A typical example was *Deinotherium*, which had a pair of tusks in the lower jaw, not the upper jaw as in modern elephants. These tusks curled round under the chin, and they may have been used for scraping bark from trees.

Massive mastodonts

Other proboscideans are termed the mastodonts, and several lineages appeared in the Miocene. One was the gomphotheres, such as *Gomphotherium* from the Miocene

(Continued on page 118.)

PLATYBELODON

This four-tusked mastodont differed from the other four-tusker, Gomphotherium *(see opposite), in having short tusks (modified canine teeth) in the upper jaw, and broad lower tusks (modified incisor teeth) in the lower jaw.* Platybelodon *is known from excellent fossilized skeletons from the Middle Miocene period of Mongolia, and it spread across northern Asia, Europe and Africa. It is generally assumed that* Platybelodon *used its shovel tusks to scrape up aquatic plants; the short upper tusks may have helped to hold the food as the trunk pushed it into the mouth.*

THE LATE MIOCENE OF EUROPE

A rainy day in southern Europe some 15 million years ago. The climate was subtropical, and the wildlife had a faintly "African" look to it, largely because conditions were wetter and the land was more heavily forested than today.

The dirk-toothed cat *Machairodus* is shown feeding on a deer (left), while the giraffid *Samotherium* and some *Hipparion* horses look on, centre bottom. The ape *Ramapithecus* shelters in a tree in the background and also on the right, high above the ground, where two kinds of elephants, the curved-tusked *Deinotherium* and the straight-tusked *Gomphotherium* seek vegetation. The carnivorous "bear-dog" *Amphicyon* lurks in the middle distance, towards the left.

The European animals of Miocene times included a variety of forms which ranged from the medium-sized cat Machairodus *(1), the horse* Hipparion *(2) and the giraffid* Samotherium *(3), to the proboscidean* Deinotherium *(4). The ape-like* Ramapithecus *(5) was relatively small, while the proboscidean* Gomphotherium *(6) and the carnivore* Amphicyon *(7) exceeded human size.*

ARSINOITHERIUM

One of the oddest heavyweight mammals, Arsinoitherium fossils have been found in Oligocene rocks in Egypt, and possible relatives come from southern Europe, Turkey and Mongolia, but the relationships of the group are a complete mystery. Arsinoitherium was a heavily-built herbivore, superficially like a rhinoceros, but not in the true rhino group. It has two vast horns, side by side, which may have been used in fighting. Its lifestyle and evolutionary position are still uncertain.

of Europe, Africa and Pakistan. It had four tusks – two uppers and two lowers – all of which stuck out forwards. Some of its relatives had flattened, shovel-like tusks that may have been used for digging up plants. These Miocene animals spread over much of the Old World and North America, and entered South America when the land bridge formed (see page 101).

The mastodonts underwent spectacular evolution in the Americas during the Pliocene and Pleistocene epochs. Indeed, it was a mastodont from Ohio which created such a furore in the late eighteenth century over the idea of extinction (see page 10).

The mastodonts retained the primitive proboscidean pattern of rounded, mound-like cusps on the cheek teeth. Another group, the mammoths (see page 131) and modern-type elephants, further elaborated the teeth as parallel-ridged, rasping devices. The ridges became higher and increased in number in mammoths and elephants, to 10-25 transverse lines. The valleys between the enamel-covered ridges filled with cement. During wear, the hard enamel was broached, and the softer internal dentine exposed. The result is a worn tooth surface that resembles a woodworker's rasping tool, with 20-50 alternating sharp ridges and valleys from front to back, running in the sequence of enamel, dentine, enamel, cement; and so on. It is difficult to think of a better grass-grinding device.

Mermaids and conies

The closest relatives of the elephants are an extremely unlikely collection of animals. The sea cows of the order Sirenia appear to be their nearest cousins. These large, fat mammals have broad horizontal tail flukes, paddle limbs and a blunt snout, somewhat like a cross between a dolphin and a tuskless walrus. They live in coastal seas and fresh waters of tropical regions, munching aquatic plants. Sightings of sea cows by early sailors are said to have given rise to mermaid stories. This seems hard to believe, unless the sailors were particularly feverish after suffering from scurvy, vermin-ridden meat and an absence of female company for many months!

The sea cows date back to the Early Eocene, but diversified mainly in the Miocene. The Miocene dugong *Dusisiren* has a downturned snout, a reduced dentition with only four cheek teeth on each side, broad thickened ribs, front limb paddles, reduced hind limbs and a whale-like tail.

The hyraxes are even less likely as relatives of elephants, although many paleontologists and biologists agree that the two groups are closely linked. These rabbit-sized animals from Africa and the Middle East are the "conies" or "rock-rabbits" of the Bible. They feed on a mixed diet, mainly plants, and betray their curious ancestry in the skeleton. Although externally the hyraxes look like earless rabbits, their skulls and wrists are elephant-like. Hyraxes date back to the Eocene; they evolved rapidly in the Oligocene and Miocene, with some being quite large, but only two genera survive today.

Bear-dogs and giant cats

The carnivorous mammals of the Miocene, which preyed on the burgeoning groups of ungulates grazing the great grasslands, nearly all belonged to the modern order Carnivora – the familiar groups of cats, dogs, weasels and their relatives. The mammalian order Carnivora dates from the Late Palaeocene and Eocene. It achieved some success in the Oligocene, after the extinction of earlier meat-eaters, but several major evolutionary lines came to greater prominence in the Miocene.

The dogs (canids) underwent a burst of adaptive radiation in the Miocene, and they are still successful today, as wolves, jackals, coyotes, foxes and domestic dogs. Their hunting style in the wild is to travel in packs and carefully

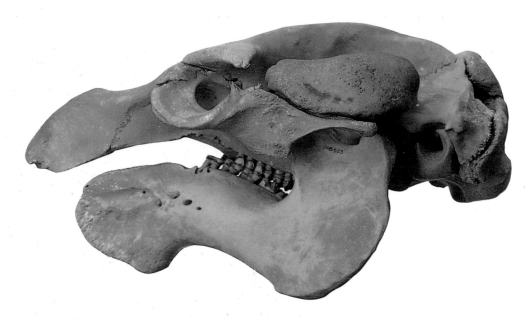

The peculiar skull of a modern manatee or "sea cow", Trichechus, *which lives in rivers bordering the Atlantic Ocean, where it feeds on aquatic plants. The jaws are largely toothless except for a few small cheek teeth, and the blunt, rounded head is attached to a bulky, seal-like body. It may seem unlikely that sailors in early days misidentified these manatees as mermaids!*

select their prey animal. They separate a youngster or an older, weak animal from the herd, and chase it, snapping at its legs to weaken it. After a chase, the prey animal usually drops from exhaustion, and then all members of the dog pack can share in the feast. This kind of pack hunting requires a degree of intelligence and a strict social structure with a clearly defined hierarchy. It is probable that it developed as a response to new sources of food – immense herds of large ungulates on the new grasslands – and it has given dogs the particular characters that make them so attractive to us as working animals and pets.

The bear-dogs, or amphicyonids, were important creatures in the Oligocene landscape (see page 67), and they continued to evolve in the Miocene. *Amphicyon*, from Miocene times in Europe, was as large as a tiger but more heavily built, rather like a bear. It hunted the slower-moving plant-eaters of its day. The amphicyonids survived into the Pliocene epoch in Africa and Eurasia, but they were eventually replaced by the true dogs, which could hunt the faster-moving ungulates more successfully.

Relatives of the dogs – the bears, raccoons and weasels – all lived successfully during Miocene times, but their fossil records are not extensive.

The cat side of carnivore evolution (see page 67) also continued in the Miocene and Pliocene. Civets and mongooses are highly successful today in the Old World, yet their fossil record is poor. The hyaenas arose in the Early Miocene in Europe, as generalized carnivores, and later

gave rise to the bone-crushing hunter-scavengers we know today in Africa. These superficially dog-like creatures are pack animals, hunting in groups, as dogs do, but their skeletons show clear affinities with the cats.

The stabbing and sabre-toothed cats rose to prominence in the Miocene and Pliocene. *Machairodus* was a typical large sabre-toothed cat of the Late Miocene and Pliocene, ranging across Old World and North America. It fed on the elephants, horses and deer that were abundant at the time.

Burrowers and gnawers

The rodents – rats, mice, beavers and porcupines – are highly successful animals today, due in no small measure to their efficient gnawing apparatus (see page 72). Certain Miocene representatives are striking, some creating elaborate burrow systems in the ground while others sprouted horns!

Modern beavers are renowned for their dam-building activities, but Oligocene and Miocene equivalents created elaborate helical burrows. The preserved burrows were found in Nebraska, USA, and they were named *Daimonelix*. The tunnels extend 2.5 metres (8½ feet) deep and each has an upper entrance pit, a middle vertical spiral and a lower living chamber. The burrow remains the same width all the way down, except for the broader living

The skeleton of a sabre-toothed cat, Smilodon, *from the famous Pleistocene tar pits of Rancho La Brea, Los Angeles, USA. This relatively slow-moving cat preyed on thick-skinned herbivores such as elephants, and relied on its amazingly long canine teeth for piercing their hides. The prey then bled to death.* Smilodon *probably did not attempt to hunt smaller, fleet-footed herbivores, or wrestle them to the ground, as lions and tigers do today.*

chamber, and the helix may curve to right or left. After the burrows were first discovered, there was some debate about the excavator; but fossilized skeletons of the beaver *Palaeocastor* were later found in place in the living chambers.

Daimonelix burrows have also been recorded from the Early Eocene, well before the oldest beaver fossils. Does this suggest that beavers are similarly ancient, or that other primitive rodents made them? It is a noteworthy fact, too, that the Eocene burrows are much simpler in construction than the Miocene ones.

The oddest rodents were the Miocene mylagaulids. *Epigaulus*, a hefty marmot-like animal from the Great Basin, USA, had broad, paddle-like hands with long claws, used for digging, and small eyes. It was probably a burrower, the eyes being small since they were of little use underground and they were protected from damage while burrowing. The oddest feature of *Epigaulus* was the pair of small horns on the snout, just in front of the eyes. Their function is a mystery, unless they were also to protect the eyes. Or they were possibly for pre-mating fights between males; some fossil specimens do not have the horns, and these may be the females.

The rodents evolved in various ways during the time of the Miocene and Pliocene. Certain lineages in South America became as big as deer. In the Old World and North America, one lineage consisted of the myomorphs – a group which included mice, rats, hamsters and voles – which today are a vast group of 1,200 species, by far the largest subgroup of rodents.

Myomorphs originated in the Eocene, but experienced their most rapid evolution only during the last five million years. They are highly adaptable animals, living in all climatic conditions, and modifying their lifestyles rapidly to exploit human habitats. Their rates of evolution are so rapid that it has been possible to disentangle complex sequences of change even within historical times, by genetic studies. Some populations of mice or voles became isolated on islands only a few hundred years ago, and already in these short spans of time, differences with their mainland relatives have emerged.

Taking to the trees

The mammalian order Primates includes lemurs, bush-babies and tarsiers, and monkeys and apes – including ourselves. The oldest known primates date from Late Cretaceous or Early Palaeocene times. The group underwent several evolutionary radiations during the time of the Palaeocene, Eocene and Oligocene epochs, giving rise

BURROWING BEAVERS

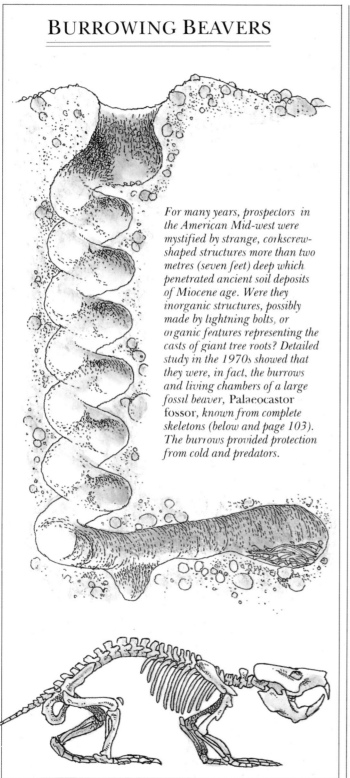

For many years, prospectors in the American Mid-west were mystified by strange, corkscrew-shaped structures more than two metres (seven feet) deep which penetrated ancient soil deposits of Miocene age. Were they inorganic structures, possibly made by lightning bolts, or organic features representing the casts of giant tree roots? Detailed study in the 1970s showed that they were, in fact, the burrows and living chambers of a large fossil beaver, Palaeocastor fossor, *known from complete skeletons (below and page 103). The burrows provided protection from cold and predators.*

A skull of the oldest ape, Aegyptopithecus, *from the Oligocene beds of Egypt. This baboon-sized animal shows some advances over monkeys, in having a relatively larger skull and no tail. Both features are characteristic of later apes, including humans.*

to a variety of extinct and surviving groups. But they experienced their greatest burst of evolution in the Miocene and Pliocene.

Primates are distinguished from other mammals by a variety of features, some connected with agility in trees – including a mobile shoulder joint, grasping hand and nails instead of claws. They also have a relatively large brain and acute eyesight, a flat face and forward-looking eyes giving binocular vision. Primates show increased parental care, involving one or a few young per pregnancy and a long period for raising the offspring.

The Palaeocene and Eocene primates were like lemurs, tarsiers and bushbabies. These living groups, and some extinct ones, are often included in the group known as "prosimians". This is to distinguish them from the more advanced cladistic group consisting of monkeys, apes and humans. Monkeys arose in the Eocene, and split into two groups, the New World monkeys and Old World monkeys. New World monkeys evolved in South America from the Oligocene and have broad flat noses and prehensile tails, which sets them apart from the Old World monkeys which have narrow noses and non-grasping tails.

Before the chimps

The apes first appeared in the Late Oligocene, but diversified dramatically during the Miocene, especially in Africa. One of the best-known early apes is *Proconsul* from Kenya. It was given this whimsical name (meaning "before Consul") in 1933, in honour of a chimpanzee named Consul who was living at London Zoo at the time. *Proconsul* had a long monkey-like body and a primitive head, but its limbs were ape-like, and it lacked a tail – a key ape feature. Many different ways of moving have been proposed for *Proconsul* over the years, ranging from almost bipedal walking, through knuckle walking (as seen in chimps and gorillas today), to full brachiation – that is, hanging and swinging hand over hand through the trees. However, it seems most likely that *Proconsul* moved along the ground on all fours and ran along large branches. The teeth are small, except for the projecting canines, and this early ape probably fed on soft fruit.

The geology of the Kenya sites which yielded *Proconsul* fossils shows that the landscape was dotted with volcanoes, rivers and flood plains. The vegetation was a mosaic of tropical forest and open woodland, with developing grasslands on the flood plains. The *Proconsul* remains were found on the forested lower slopes of the volcanoes and on the flood plains, but not in the wetter habitats around the rivers which have produced fossils of crocodilians, elephants and rhinos. As many as three species of *Proconsul* may have coexisted in Kenya at the time, together with four or five other monkeys and apes.

During the Early Miocene, Africa was still effectively an island (see page 86). About 18 million years ago it came into contact with Eurasia, and it was possible for land animals to cross both ways. Middle and Late Miocene apes such as *Sivapithecus* were thus able to leave Africa, and specimens have been found as far away as Hungary, Greece, Turkey, India, Pakistan and China. *Sivapithecus* was larger than *Proconsul* and broadly like a modern orang-utan. It had heavy jaws and strong teeth with thick enamel, which suggests a diet of tough vegetation. A close relative of *Sivapithecus* was *Gigantopithecus*, which lived into

Pleistocene times in China. Males of this huge ape may have reached a height of 2.5 metres (8½ feet) and a weight of 270 kilograms (almost 600 pounds). Remnant populations may be the source of old legends about yetis in Central Asia and the bigfoot of North America, although it is exceptionally doubtful that *Gigantopithecus* survives to this day.

Open grasslands and the origin of humans

We like to think that our main human characteristic is our large brain, giving high intelligence. Surely this is the reason for our differentiation from the apes, and the basis of our great success? Indeed, paleoanthropologists held this general view until quite recently. However, fossil evidence now suggests that bipedalism – the ability to walk

PROCONSUL

One of the most famous early apes, this creature is the centre of many arguments about the ancestry of humans. Proconsul was named in the 1930s on the basis of African specimens, from the Early Miocene of Kenya. Since then, about eight species from its genus have been named from around the Mediterranean and in East Africa. Until recently, many paleoanthropologists thought Proconsul *was a true ancestor of humans, but it is now seen as an ape, on the common line to modern apes and humans. It was essentially quadrupedal and ground-dwelling, but it was probably quite agile in large branches.*

on the hind limbs – was the crucial adaptation that set the human line apart. The stimulus for bipedalism is thought to have been the growth of open savannah grasslands in Africa.

Some 15-10 million years ago, the great tropical forests that covered much of Africa began to retreat to their present distribution, mainly in the Congo Basin. Areas to the north became desert, as the Sahara, and lands to the east and south changed to open savannah, arid grasslands with only scattered trees.

Our current view is that the Miocene apes on the western side of the African continent gave rise to the modern African apes, the tree-dwelling chimps and gorillas. It is thought that the apes to the east and south became human beings. A key adaptation to survival in the open plains was the ability to stand upright, to see danger, and then to escape from it by fast running. No longer could our ancestors rely on camouflage and tree-climbing for safety.

Once bipedalism had evolved, it allowed various possibilities, such as using the hands to carry things or to make tools. These were not the evolutionary stimuli that led to bipedalism, but consequences. Manual dexterity, tool-making and other forms of manufacture were enabled by the acquisition of bipedalism. Arguably, the expanded brain followed this trend, being required to deal with the new possibilities. Hence, our intelligence may derive more from the need of our Late Miocene ancestors to escape predation by standing upright, than from any peculiar or mystical benefits of having a large brain.

Truly human

The paleontological evidence supports the above view. The oldest remains of human-like creatures are a series of footprints in a layer of volcanic ash, deposited 3.75 million years ago in Tanzania. They are the prints of an adult and child walking fully bipedally, upright on two feet. The first truly human bones are dated at slightly over three million years old, from the Late Pliocene. They are the skeleton of a female hominid nicknamed Lucy, more properly called *Australopithecus afarensis*, found in the early 1970s. She was an adult, but only about 1.2 metres (4 feet) tall. Her skull was still very ape-like, with a rather small brain, but her limbs show every sign of efficient bipedalism.

Australopithecus survived in Africa until about one million years ago, well into the Pleistocene (see chapter six), by which time members of our own genus *Homo* had also come on the scene. It was only at this time, between two and one million years ago, that there was a significant jump in brain

The most famous image of a human fossil from the 1970s – "Lucy". She is the best specimen of Australopithecus afarensis, *the oldest human, collected from Ethiopia. The remains show nearly half of the skeleton of a tiny adult, about 1.2 metres (48 inches) tall. The skull shows that Lucy had relatively human brain-body proportions, and her legs, knees and feet were adapted for fully upright human walking.*

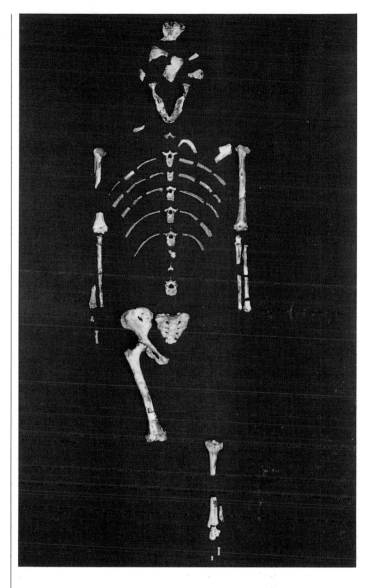

size to something like modern proportions. This was associated with evidence of tool-making and more complex lifestyles.

Looking back on the story of mammalian evolution in the Miocene and Pliocene, it seems to have been directed by the dramatic spread of a major new habitat, the great grasslands. On all continents, there is clear evidence that the evolution of herbivores and carnivores alike followed new pathways as a result. And this seems to be as true for primates as for ungulates. It is becoming clear that we owe our own origins to the replacement of the lush African forests by grasslands in the Mid and Late Miocene.

CHAPTER SIX

THE ICE AGES

The last two million years of evolution have been marked by some spectacular and unusual mammals, and by key stages of human evolution. Events during this time were largely controlled by the dramatic climatic changes that were involved in the great ice ages. These affected northern continents in particular, but repercussions were felt worldwide. The ice ages were characterized by woolly rhinos, mammoths, cave bears and Neanderthal people in the cold northern lands, and by yet more giant creatures in southern continents.

The Pleistocene epoch (2 million years to about 10,000 years ago) is marked by at least seven separate ice ages, during which the ice cap covering the North Pole expanded southwards and blanketed parts of Europe as far as England, Germany, northern Asia and the northern USA. The advancing cold also induced the expansion of small ice caps outwards from the Alps, the Rockies and the Himalayas. How did these dramatic events occur?

The Pleistocene ice ages are not the only ones on record. The world's climate has gone through great cycles of change, sometimes warmer and sometimes cooler. In fact, there had been major cooling phases and ice advances in the Ordovician (440 million years ago) and the Carboniferous/Permian (290 million years ago), as well as some other less completely known events. Today's climates are rather cooler than has been the norm in the history of the Earth, and we may still be in part of a Pleistocene ice age.

For most of geological time, it seems that there were no

The Altschgletscher (opposite), the longest glacier in Europe, sliding down the Alps in Switzerland. Note the medial and lateral moraines, strings of rocks and earth within the centre and sides of the glacier respectively, and stripped rocky terrain on either side. Many times during the last two million years, glaciers have advanced outwards from the Alps, and south from Greenland, to cover much of northern Europe and Canada. These Ice Ages profoundly affected the evolution of mammals.

ice caps at the poles. Now about one tenth of the Earth's surface is covered with ice. At the height of the Pleistocene ice ages, this figure was nearer one-third. Ice caps of these sizes lock up a great deal of the planet's water: some 26 million cubic kilometres (three-quarters of the world's fresh water) today, and 76 million cubic kilometres in the Pleistocene.

Early in the nineteenth century, geologists knew nothing of major ice ages in the past. They observed many of the pieces of evidence, but misinterpreted them. One of the commonest phenomena caused by ice fields is that great boulders of rock are moved many kilometres from their source and dumped where the ice melts. These great boulders, or "erratics" as they are known, occur all over Europe. They were explained at first as having been moved along by Noah's flood. During the early nineteenth century, many geologists argued that these boulders had been carried in the bottoms of small glaciers and dropped on to the surface, where they now lie. This can happen, and the rocks are called dropstones. However, there were so many erratics, and many lay high in the hills, that this could not explain them all.

The ice-age landscape

Finally, in the 1830s, the great Swiss geologist Louis Agassiz recognized that the erratic boulders had been moved along by glaciers of enormous size – glaciers that had advanced south over northern Europe and outwards from the Alps (which he could study in his own country). Agassiz and others then interpreted many other superficial features of

cold climates, while hippos and long-tusked elephants wandering through the English countryside show that climates during some phases were considerably warmer than today. Fossil pollen and beetles give an even clearer picture.

Terrestrial plants produce large amounts of pollen just before the seeds are set. Much of it falls into ponds or onto the soil. Every plant produces a different kind of pollen, and under the microscope the pollen grains can be readily distinguished. Since the Pleistocene epoch covers only the last two million years, virtually all the pollen found from this time belongs to modern plant species, and it can be identified with confidence. This is the key to its use in determining Pleistocene climates. Pollen can indicate precise climatic conditions, since most plants have preferred ranges of temperature and humidity.

During the onset of a glaciation, the pollen types show a typical cycle of replacement of plant communities. Zones of vegetation characteristic of warmer, equable conditions migrate away south, while colder tundra-type vegetation comes down from the north. The glacial advances and retreats probably took several thousands of years, and this allowed time for the plants to change in a progressive way, without catastrophic extinctions. A typical cycle recorded across central Europe is as follows: mixed deciduous forest; boreal conifer forest; birch forest; tundra with lichens; polar "desert" with no plants; continental ice sheet. As the ice sheet retreated, the cycle would run in reverse.

Beetles have also proved to be extremely useful climatic

the scenery in northern Europe for what they really were: conclusive proof of a blanket of moving ice in the fairly recent past. These features include U-shaped valleys carved by advancing glaciers; hanging valleys left well above the now-deepened main valley; moraines, which are the deposits of ground-up rock dumped at the front of a melting glacier as it receded; drumlins, or rounded piles of sand deposited beneath a thin glacier; and scratched rock surfaces where boulders borne by the glacier have made long parallel gouges in the bedrock.

These features were all readily observed by the early geologists, and their evidence has been supplemented by more sophisticated proof of the great glaciations. For example, Scandinavia and northern Scotland are rising out of the sea at a measurable rate. This is known as "isostatic glacial rebound". The great weight of ice that lay over these areas pressed the land down, and it is still recovering and rising back to its correct level, at which the Earth's crust will achieve balance. Some regions have already risen 100 metres (330 feet) or more since the retreat of the last ice sheet, 10,000 years ago.

From warm to cold: pollen and beetles

Geologists and paleontologists now have sophisticated ways of reconstructing in detail the Pleistocene climates of different parts of the world. Fossil mammals, of course, give useful indications. Mammoths and woolly rhinos point to

A perched erratic block from East Greenland. Erratic blocks are rocks that have been transported some distance by a moving glacier, and then dumped at the side or end of the glacier when it melted and retreated. Erratics are common evidence of the former presence of glaciers in northern Europe and Canada.

Photomicrograph of fossil pollen grains from spruce trees, from a Pleistocene site in Michigan, USA, found in association with a mastodon. Pollen grains like these are commonly found in Pleistocene deposits, and they indicate the plants present, and therefore the climate at the time.

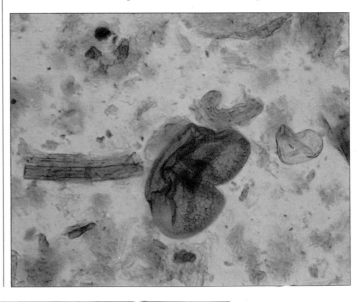

indicators for the Pleistocene, giving an independent picture of events. Many groups of beetles are just as temperature-dependent as plants, with some species preferring a cold climate and others typical of warm conditions. Beetles are often well preserved in Pleistocene soils, and they can be identified even from parts of their genitalia, which tend to survive best! The Pleistocene species are nearly all still alive today, so their climatic preferences are known. Therefore, sequences of climatic change can be drawn up for any section of Pleistocene soil, based on independent evidence of pollen and beetles.

A third technique for determining temperature changes is geochemical: the measurement of changes in oxygen isotope ratios. Oxygen is present in sea water as two chemical forms, or isotopes. These are incorporated into the shells of single-celled planktonic creatures called foraminiferans, in the same proportions as the isotopes occur in the surrounding sea water. The proportions of the isotopes follow temperature changes, more particularly the volumes of glacial ice. Detailed graphs have been drawn from isotope contents of deep-sea sediment cores which contain the shells of billions of foraminiferans. These show about 18 cold episodes during the Pleistocene, one every 100,000 years or so, and seven of these appear to have been linked to major ice advances.

Glacials and interglacials

The first major glacial episode began about 1.6 million years ago, when ice advanced southwards over northern Europe and northern North America. This is termed the Nebraska or Donau glacial, depending upon which side of the Atlantic you are. The ice retreated for a long phase before the second major glacial episode, known as the Kansan or Günz glacial, began about 900,000 years ago. At least three more glacial phases are recognized: the Mindel or Illinoian-2 about 500,000 years ago, the Riss or Wisconsinan-1 about 200,000 years ago, and the Wurm or Wisconsinan-2 about 80,000-10,000 years ago. Earlier episodes have been hard to date, and other minor ones doubtless existed in between.

The glacials seem to have begun relatively slowly but finished more rapidly, within a few thousand years. The intervening periods, or interglacials, are also recognizable phases. They have been given names that relate to the areas in which their fossils are best preserved, or where major physical effects are seen. Both glacials and interglacials were characterized by very different kinds of plants and animals, as we have seen.

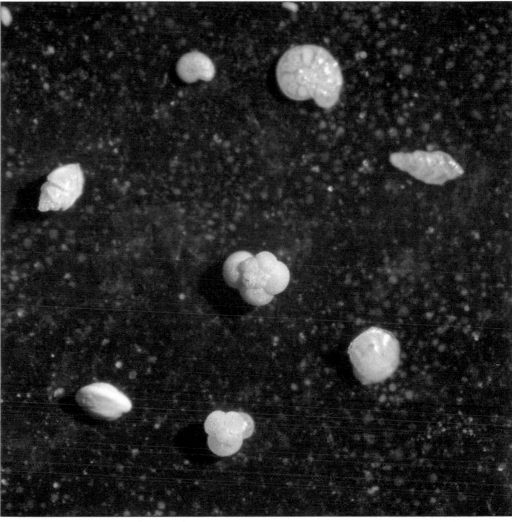

Calcareous shells of foraminifera from marine sediments. These microscopic, single-celled protozoans develop tiny protective shells, many superficially like snail shells. They float as plankton in the surface waters of the sea, feeding on minute algae. When they die, the shells sink to the sea floor, forming thick layers of limestone. "Forams" give clear evidence of the date of marine sediments, and of the climate.

Along the edges of the great continental ice sheets were tundra, areas of frozen soil supporting only low grasses, lichens and small bushes. Yet these seemingly inhospitable landscapes were able to support a diverse collection of mammals such as large woolly rhinos, mammoths, cattle and reindeer, which fed on the grasses, leaves and lichens exposed in shallow snow. Some of these animals migrated south during the winter while others, such as the cave bear and some rodents, hibernated.

During the interglacials, plants and animals adapted to warmer climates spread into Europe from North Africa and the Middle East, and into northern North America from the southern USA and Central America. The plants supported a variety of African-type elephants, pigs, bison, deer, hippos, cave lions, brown bears and hyaenas (Continued on page 130.)

ICE AGE MAMMALS IN EUROPE

A scene during the last European Ice Age, some 40,000 years ago, with a Neanderthal hunter moving quietly through the woods (right). All the animals are adapted to cold conditions. The musk oxen *Moschus*, giant Irish deer *Megaloceros*, horses *Equus*, mammoth *Mammuthus*, and woolly rhinoceros *Elasmotherium* are all at middle left, feeding on the stunted grasses, lichens and low bushes of the open tundra. Behind the trees are reindeer *Rangifer*, wolves *Canis*, and a cave bear *Ursus spelaeus*. Smaller animals include the snow hare *Lepus* in the right foreground, and also being eaten by the lynx *Lynx*. Birds present include the raven *Corvus*.

The world as it was then.

Ice age animals shown in the scene are Lepus *(1),* Moschus *(2),* Rangifer *(3),* Canis *(4),* Ursus *(5),* Mammuthus *(6),* Lynx *(7),* Elasmotherium *(8),* Megaloceros *(9),* Corvus *(10), and of course* Homo sapiens neanderthalensis *(11).*

in northern Europe. In North America, animals of the interglacials included elephants, horses, giant ground sloths, pronghorns, dire wolves and sabre-toothed cats. Many of these typical glacial and interglacial creatures are now extinct.

What caused the ice ages?

We know that ice ages have occurred frequently in the history of the Earth, and particularly during the past two million years. But why did they happen?

The causes may be astronomical. One theory relates to the "precession of the equinoxes" – the fact that there is a slight wobble in the axis of the Earth's rotation, which is caused by the gravitational pull of the Sun and the Moon on the Earth. The precession occurs over a time cycle of 22,000 years. The tilt of the Earth affects the amount of sunlight reaching polar regions at different stages of the cycle, and a particularly dark time at the North Pole may have induced a sharp drop in temperature.

Other ice-age theories are that the uplift of the Alps triggered large glaciers there, and so lowered global temperatures; or there was a drop in the output of energy from the Sun; or the formation of the Isthmus of Panama three million years ago redirected the oceanic Gulf Stream current northwards and increased rainfall, and hence water supply, to the north polar ice cap. Although it is interesting to speculate, there is no strong evidence either way for these theories.

The dramatic spread of the ice caps southwards during each major glacial is explained by "synergistic" effects following the initial trigger of a cold snap. Once ice starts to spread, this induces a further fall in temperature and the formation of yet more ice. This kind of self-reinforcing process could have blanketed much of Europe and North America with ice, following only a modest drop in polar temperatures. The main reason for this synergistic effect is that ice reflects the Sun's light and heat, and therefore produces a zone of cooling. A patch of ice reflects more sunlight than an equivalent area of land or sea, and the cooling effect tends to make the patch grow, especially if it lies on land.

Despite all of the research and theorizing, however, we are still not sure why the ice ages occurred, or whether they will return in the future.

EXTENT OF THE ICE SHEET

At its maximum, the north polar ice (shown on the globe, right) extended south over Canada and into Michigan and New York State in the USA, and over much of England, Germany, central Europe and the USSR.

Subsidiary ice caps moved out from the Rockies, Alps and Himalayas. As the ice advanced and retreated, the vegetation zones moved ahead of it (see below). Closest to the ice front was the polar desert, devoid of

vegetation. At even greater distances were tundra, with tiny buried plants; then low bushes, birch trees and conifers; and finally temperate deciduous woodland.

deciduous mixed forest

boreal conifer forest

birch forest

S

N

Paris

Hamburg

Stockholm

birch forest

tundra

polar desert

continental ice sheet

Ice-age elephants

Mammoths are probably the most potent images of the Pleistocene landscape, and they spread from Africa over much of Europe and Asia, and later to North America. The woolly mammoth is exceptionally well represented in the fossil record, by tonnes of bones, tusks and even nearly complete carcasses preserved for thousands of years in the frozen tundra of Siberia and Alaska. The mammoth was 2.8 metres (9 feet) tall, and covered by an 8-centimetre (3½-inch) layer of fat beneath the skin, as well as a coat of shaggy red hair. The broad sweeping tusks may have been used to clear snow from this beast's food of grasses.

The deep-freeze conditions of Siberia are so exceptional that dozens of woolly mammoth specimens were located in the eighteenth and nineteenth centuries. Sadly, often the tusks were removed and the flesh left to rot in the air. At one time, more ivory came from "subfossil" mammoths than from modern elephants! The flesh of these frozen mammoths can still be eaten, as was done at a great scientific banquet in Russia during the last century. The meat was edible, but not really of gourmet standard! The preservation of some woolly mammoth specimens was so good that their own last meals could be found in their stomachs, and even in the mouth – indicating that death came suddenly. Mammoths lived side by side with humans; they died out only 12,000 years ago in Europe and 10,000 years ago in North America.

Various other elephants lived during the Pleistocene, including the mastodon in North America (see page 115). This was a forest-browser, rather smaller than the great mammoth, and equipped with very different teeth which still retained the primitive pattern of large, rounded cusps. The mastodon died out 8,000 years ago.

Giants of the north

The woolly rhinoceros, *Coelodonta*, was a typical companion of the mammoth in northern Europe and Asia, with its shaggy red coat and a pair of long horns on its snout. Other European creatures included relatives of mammals that still dwell on the tundra, including reindeer, musk-oxen, lemmings, hares, wolves and bears.

The extinct Irish deer, *Megaloceros*, was common throughout much of Europe. It was larger than its modern relatives, and famous for the enormous span of its antlers (see page

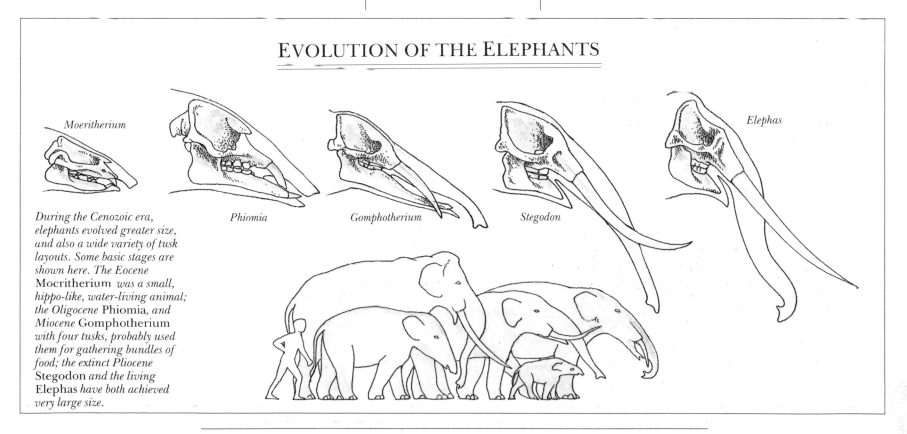

EVOLUTION OF THE ELEPHANTS

Moeritherium

Phiomia

Gomphotherium

Stegodon

Elephas

During the Cenozoic era, elephants evolved greater size, and also a wide variety of tusk layouts. Some basic stages are shown here. The Eocene Mocritherium *was a small, hippo-like, water-living animal; the Oligocene* Phiomia, *and Miocene* Gomphotherium *with four tusks, probably used them for gathering bundles of food; the extinct Pliocene* Stegodon *and the living* Elephas *have both achieved very large size.*

110). There were also giant cattle, the aurochs, which were ancestors of modern cattle and lived in central Europe until a few centuries ago.

Many of these mammals were larger than their modern relatives. This was also true of areas farther south that were not glaciated, but still probably suffered from some cold. The African warthog *Afrochoerus* was twice the size of its modern relatives, and the Asian rhinoceros *Elasmotherium* was nearly twice the length of living cousins. This is not unexpected, since large size is a way of resisting the cold. The surface area of a large animal relative to its bulk or weight is much lower than in a small animal, and less surface reduces the rate of heat loss. Of course, many of these animals also had thick fat layers and shaggy fur to assist insulation.

The mammals of the North American ice ages share similar characters to their European counterparts. They included large shaggy mastodons, mammoths, elk, deer and cattle, as well as representatives of modern tundra-zone mammals. Some of the best-known mammals, however, come from warmer conditions in the Late Pleistocene, about 11,000 years ago. They were preserved in the La Brea tar pits in Los Angeles, California, USA.

Trapped in tar

The tar pits of La Brea are natural seeps of heavy oil, which have formed deep lakes of gooey black tar. In the Late Pleistocene, leaves and twigs coated the surface and gave the appearance of solid ground, while water gathered in hollows. Hence many mammals and other animals were tempted onto this treacherous surface. Elephants, horses and giant ground sloths came down to drink, but soon

The skeleton of a woolly mammoth, Mammuthus primigenius *(above), the most potent image of the Ice Ages. Herds of these elephants roamed over Europe and northern Asia, and many preserved remains have been found – some even with hair and flesh intact. To reach food it swept its head from side to side, using its vast curving tusks to scrape snow from the ground.*

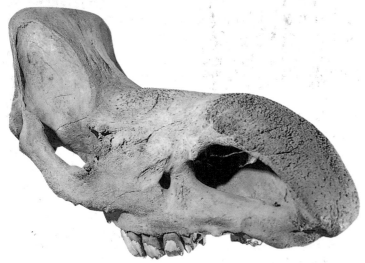

A fossil skull of the woolly rhinoceros Coelodonta antiquitatis *(above), from the Tunguska River, Siberia, USSR. There is no nose horn since that characteristic piece of rhinoceros equipment is not really horn at all, but a highly compacted mass of matted hair. Hence, it is not preserved with the bones as part of the fossilized remains.*

A reconstruction of a straight-tusked mastodont succumbing to the tar pits in Rancho La Brea, Los Angeles, USA (right). Dozens of exquisitely preserved skeletons of such elephants have been disinterred from the tar.

The sabre-toothed cat Smilodon *from the Rancho La Brea tar pits. The knife-like sabre teeth were actually rather blunt at the ends, as can be seen here, and so they could not have been used for simple puncturing or slicing of the prey's skin. It is now thought that* Smilodon *grasped loose skin on the neck of its victim, and shook and pulled until it could close its jaws and tear out a great chunk of flesh. The hapless prey animal ran off, closely followed by the cat, which waited until the victim bled to death.*

began to sink in. Predators were attracted by their struggles, and they in turn became trapped. Sabre-toothed cats, dire wolves and vultures are among the most common remains. Humans were also in the area at the time, but they seem to have had the sense to keep clear!

The tar pits have been excavated by paleontologists for many years, and thousands of perfectly preserved skeletons have been brought out. These include 2,000 skeletons of *Smilodon*, the best-known sabre-toothed cat (see page 67).

Life on the southern continents

The Pleistocene mammals of Africa were comparable to those today. The dramatic changes seen in the northern continents do not seem to have occurred, probably because climatic changes were less marked. There were elephants,

pigs, rhinos, hippos, antelopes, camels, apes and humans, just as today.

South American Pleistocene mammals did include some unusual creatures, such as toxodonts, giant ground sloths and glyptodonts. There were also invaders from the north, among them Imperial mammoths, sabre-toothed cats, horses, deer, wolves and bears.

Pleistocene mammals found in Australia, such as diprotodonts, giant kangaroos and marsupial "lions", were all similarly striking.

There has been no mention yet of New Zealand, which never acquired any Australasian marsupials. Indeed, these twin islands seem to have been devoid of mammals altogether. The only large animals were birds, including various flightless forms – particularly the moas. They were

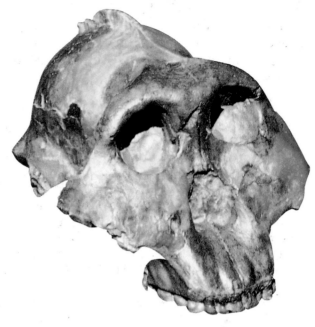

A skull of Australopithecus robustus, *found in the early 1960s by Louis B Leakey on the eastern side of Lake Rudolf, Kenya. It was known affectionately as "Zinj", based on its first-given name of* Zinjanthropus, *and also as "Nutcracker man" because of the powerful jaws. The heavy brow ridges and prolonged snout are both primitive features.*

intriguing notion of three or four species of human-like creatures living side by side, something we cannot comprehend today when there is only one species, *Homo sapiens.* It would be fascinating to observe how these rather different humans behaved when they encountered one another.

Human evolution took on a new impetus one million years ago, when the first worldwide species appeared – *Homo erectus.* The oldest fossil specimens come from East Africa, showing that this was where the species first lived. They are of a hominid up to 1.8 metres (6 feet) tall, with a brain size of about 850 cubic centimetres. *Homo erectus* had spread to north Africa by one million years ago, China and Java by 800,000 years ago, and Europe by 500,000 years ago. The Chinese remains have even larger brains, at 900-1,100 cubic centimetres, and we have excellent evidence that they were social people who lived in caves and cooked with fire. They also made tools, the Acheulian and Palaeolithic (Old Stone Age) types.

And so to the dominant

Modern humans, *Homo sapiens*, have a flat face and a brain size averaging 1,360 cubic centimetres. We seem to have evolved from *Homo erectus* in Africa or the Middle East, some time between 400,000 and 100,000 years ago. There is dispute over various transitional skulls that could belong to either species.

A side branch of *Homo sapiens* entered Europe and became adapted to the cold of the last glacial episodes, from 100,000 to 30,000 years ago. They were the Neanderthal people, given subspecies rank as *Homo sapiens neanderthalensis.* They were definitely members of our own species, but were often portrayed as dimwitted cave dwellers, wearing shaggy loin cloths and carrying massive clubs with which they beat each other senseless. Their intelligence, it is said, was low, with a receding forehead and a shuffling, slouching gait.

a diverse group, some much larger than ostriches, that seem to have been ecological equivalents of the ungulates and kangaroos elsewhere. Sadly, they were driven to extinction in historical times by human intervention. There is also more than a suspicion that humans were behind the downfall of other spectacular late Pleistocene animals, as we will see below.

The coming of humans

Humans originated some five or six million years ago, in Africa. A sparse fossil record shows that these early humans were small-brained, bipedal animals, *Australopithecus* (see page 123), that lived at least from four to one million years ago. When did the first "brainy" human come on the scene?

A lower jaw, and other skull and skeletal remains, were found in 1960 and 1963 in the famous Olduvai Gorge, Kenya, by the equally famous paleoanthropologist, Louis Leakey. They represent probably the oldest species of our own genus, *Homo.* This being was still small by our standards, about 1.3 metres (4⅓ feet) tall, but had a brain size of 650-800 cubic centimetres – a great advance over the 400-550 cubic centimetres of *Australopithecus.* The Olduvai hominid (member of the human group) was named *Homo habilis,* meaning "handy man" because of its large brain size and the possibility that it made tools.

The remains of *Homo habilis* are dated as 2.5-1.5 million years ago, and they have been found in association with fossils of several species of *Australopithecus.* This begs the

A set of four key skulls in human evolution: from left to right these are Homo sapiens, Homo erectus, Homo habilis *and* Australopithecus robustus. *The lower jaws of each are set to the side. The order of evolution is from right to left; showing the trends of an enlarging braincase, loss of the midline crest, and flattening of the face.*

Excavation of a mammoth, nicknamed "Elmer", in south-eastern Michigan, USA. This is a typical jumble of huge bones and tusks, all relatively well preserved, but presenting a headache for the collectors because of the great size of the specimens. The remains must be dug out, protected in plaster, shipped to a museum, cleaned and studied, and stored. The two great curved tusks are in the middle of the picture.

The evidence is now very much against this view, however. Neanderthals were stockily built, just as were most cold-adapted mammals, but they had our own brain size and they skilfully made a wide range of tools, clothes and houses, known as the Mousterian culture.

Neanderthals disappeared with the retreat of the most recent ice in Europe. The modern-type *Homo sapiens* that had existed in Africa and the Middle East for some time moved into Europe, bringing more advanced tools and the cave art of the Upper Palaeolithic, or New Stone Age, culture.

Modern *Homo sapiens sapiens* spread worldwide from 40,000 years ago, reaching eastern Asia at that time, and travelling to south-western Asia and Australia by about 33,000 years ago. They moved on to North America (via Siberia and Alaska) possibly as early as 40,000 years ago,

but certainly by 11,500 years ago. This great spread of our human ancestors coincides with major mass extinctions among the late Pleistocene mammals; and scientists have long wondered if the two events were linked.

The greatest mass extinction?

About 12,000 to 10,000 years ago, mammals on all continents suffered drastic changes. In North America, almost three-quarters of large mammals (some 33 genera) died out, including all of the elephants, tapirs, peccaries, camels, ground sloths and glyptodonts, as well as various predators and deer. In South America, 46 genera died out (four-fifths of the total), including ground sloths, glyptodonts, many rodents, sabre-toothed cats, wolves, peccaries, camels, deer, litopterns, notoungulates, horses and mastodonts (see page 101). The last four major groups disappeared entirely from this continent.

In Australia, major extinctions occurred between 40,000 and 15,000 years ago. Some 55 species vanished, including echidnas, marsupial carnivores, wombats, diprotodonts, kangaroos and wallabies. In addition a large lizard, the tortoise *Meiolania*, a giant snake and three birds also disappeared from fossil records.

In Europe, on the other hand, the losses were less severe. The woolly rhino, mammoth and giant deer died out, but others such as the horse, hippo, musk ox, hyaena and saiga antelope simply contracted their ranges to more favourable parts of the world. Extinctions in Africa and Asia at this time were similarly modest.

Paleontologists attribute these extinctions to a number of causes, and their discussions have separated the experts into two main camps. One explanation is that climates and environments changed rapidly as the ice sheets retreated; large mammals, in particular, were vulnerable to such disturbances within a complex community of plants and animals.

The second view is that increasing and spreading human populations wiped out the larger mammals by hunting, the so-called "overkill hypothesis". The timing is right for this more violent view. Modern humans travelled around the world between 40,000 and 10,000 years ago, and they hunted large animals on all continents. These new predators may have been fatal to the large marsupials of Australia, the elephants of North America, and the restricted South American mammals.

At present, the evidence seems to be equally balanced on both sides. The time scale of human movements suits the view of the "overkillers", and they point out that severe

EXTINCTION OF ELEPHANTS

The elephants suffered as badly as any mammal group from the Late Pleistocene extinctions. During the past seven million years (Late Miocene, Pliocene, Pleistocene), true elephants evolved into 15 or more lineages, nearly worldwide, with representatives in Africa, Asia, Europe and North America. Most of these died out only a few tens of thousands of years ago, leaving only two rather precarious survivors, Loxodonta africana *in Africa, and* Elephas maximus *in Asia. Note the differences between the two skulls below.*

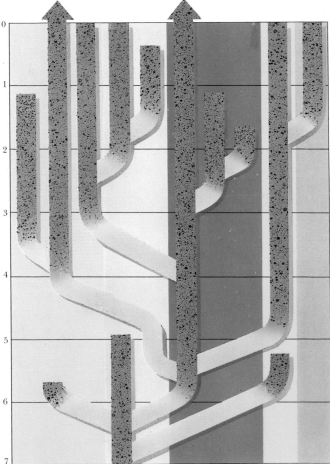

million years ago

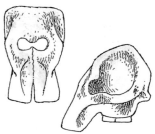

Loxodonta africana
(African elephant)

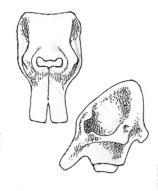

Elephas maximus
(Indian elephant)

climatic changes might have killed off the smaller mammals involved, as well as the mammals of the Old World which seemed to suffer low levels of extinction.

On the other hand, the "climatists" point out that there is almost no archeological evidence for the numerous kill sites that must have existed. In addition, humans entered North America and Australia long before the majority of extinctions took place.

Keystone herbivores

The truth of the matter could well be a combination of both viewpoints. Such a compromise would remove much of the fun of scientific controversy! However, a third theory has been proposed recently, which appears to combine both overkill and climatic deterioration. This is the "keystone herbivore" hypothesis.

The idea is that very large herbivores, those weighing over one tonne, disappeared first. Their extinction led to major changes in vegetation, which in turn led to the loss of smaller herbivores. Large herbivores today, such as elephants, rhinos and hippos, have a tremendous impact upon the plants in their landscape. Elephants knock down trees and create openings in forests. If these large herbivores are removed, the forest clearings close up and short grasslands become rank and wooded. This means smaller grazers such as antelope, cattle, pigs, camels and horses, are gradually squeezed out.

The keystone herbivore hypothesis contends that humans hunted the large herbivores to extinction in the Americas, Europe and Australia. With these big "keystone" species gone, the habitat changed drastically, and dozens of moderately-sized mammals died out as a result.

Mammals and the future

Our own species probably had some influence on the late Pleistocene extinctions, but the extent of that influence is not yet known. However, *Homo sapiens* has since had many other dramatic effects on the Earth.

All living humans are related to each other, and our common history dates back only a blink of the eye, in geological time. Genetic and molecular studies confirm the archeological evidence, that modern humans can be traced back to a single ancestral group living in Africa 100,000 years ago. This means all the physical, social and cultural differences between human groups, that we think of as so important, have developed in a short time.

Major cultural and technological advances came relatively quickly as modern *Homo sapiens* became established

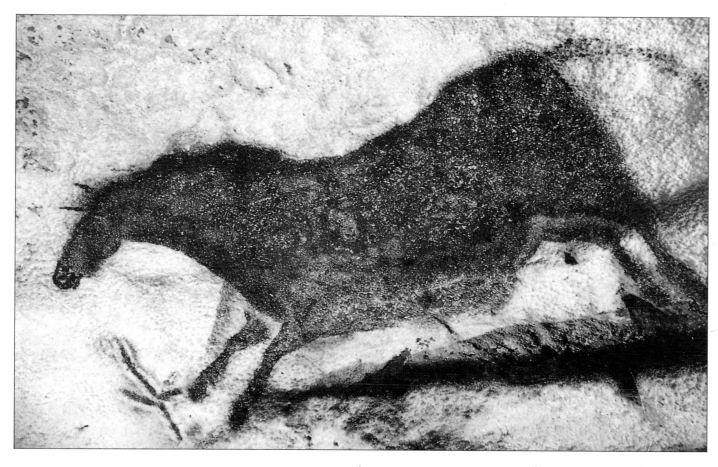

The invention of art was an important milestone in the origin of civilization. Humans began using their hands as long ago as two million years, to make stone tools, but the more imaginative or "frivolous" use of manual skills began only about 35,000 years ago, when the first crude pieces of art were completed. More elaborate cave paintings, such as this splendid running horse from the Lascaux Cave in southern France, date back only 15,000 years. Such works indicate powers of imagination and reflection, and hint at religious rituals.

worldwide. The oldest art dates from 35,000 years ago, and farming began more than 10,000 years ago, in the Middle East. The domestication of sheep, goats and cattle, and the cultivation of wheat, barley, lentils, peas and other crops, led to the first truly permanent settlements.

Further changes, brought on by the development of agriculture, were means of exchanging goods, division of labour, advances in social structures and language, and many other features of cooperative existence. Global populations began to increase about 10,000 years ago from a previously steady level of perhaps 10 million to ever higher and higher numbers, as vast areas of wild land came under the plough and the cow, and agriculture allowed more and more food to be produced.

As we look back over our evolution, the appearance of major advances seems to have accelerated towards the present: bipedalism 10-5 million years ago, an enlarged brain 3-2 million years ago, stone tools 2 million years ago, wide geographic distribution 1 million years ago, fire 500,000 years ago, art 35,000 years ago, agriculture and global population increase 10,000 years ago, industrialization some 200 years ago, telecommunications 100 years ago, and space travel 30 years ago. The rate of population increase follows a similar ever-accelerating trend, rising from an annual rate of 0.1 per cent in stone-age times, to 0.3 per cent in the eighteenth century, to 2.0 per cent and still rising today.

The massive increase in our numbers has driven many mammalian species to extinction – if not in late Pleistocene times, then certainly in the past 300 years: Steller's sea cow, the Tasmanian wolf (thylacine), the quagga, the aurochs, the Arizona jaguar, the Caribbean monk seal, the Barbary lion, and dozens more. Indeed, 19 mammal species have disappeared in three centuries, and nine of these during this century. At this increasing rate, we shall kill off another five species of mammals by the year 2000, and another 20 by 2100, until all wild species – except perhaps rats and mice – have gone by the year 2500. This is evidence for the impressive success of *Homo sapiens*, but also a stark warning of the folly of the so-called "wise human".

GLOSSARY

Certain technical terms are used in different parts of the book. Their meanings are given here.

A

Adaptive radiation: the rapid evolutionary expansion of a group, either after a *mass extinction*, or as a result of the acquisition of a new character.

Amniotes: the group including reptiles, birds and mammals; those that possess the *amniotic egg*.

Amniotic egg: the closed egg with a protective cover (shell) and complex membranes inside.

Angular: the bone in the lower jaw of reptiles at the bottom and back of the jaw; becomes the *ectotympanic* in mammals.

Arboreal: tree-living.

Articular: the bone at the very back of the lower jaw in reptiles; becomes the *malleus* in mammals.

Auditory ossicles: the small bones within the middle ear that transmit sound vibrations from the ear drum to the inner ear.

B

Bipedal: walking on two legs only.

Browsing: feeding on low bushes and trees.

C

Canines: the long pointed teeth between the *incisors* and the *cheek teeth*.

Carnassials: the pointed flesh-shredding teeth of certain carnivorous mammals.

Carnivore: a meat-eater.

Cement: the material that fixes a tooth into its socket.

Cheek teeth: the molars and premolars, or teeth behind the canines used for grinding or shredding food.

Cladogram: a branching diagram based upon an analysis of characters that reflects *phylogeny*.

Continental drift: the movement of continents and ocean floors relative to each other through geological time.

Coprolite: fossilized excrement.

Cusps: pointed cutting and grinding structures on mammalian *cheek teeth*.

Cynodonts: the carnivorous mammal-like reptiles that include the ancestors of mammals.

D

Dentary: the main element in the lower jaw of reptiles, and the sole element in that of mammals; bears teeth.

Dentine: the soft bone-like material that makes up the bulk of the interior of a tooth.

Diapsids: the "two-arched" reptiles, such as lizards, snakes, crocodilians, dinosaurs.

Diastema: a gap between the *canine tooth* and the cheek teeth often found in herbivorous mammals.

E

Ecospace: the portion of the physical and biological environment occupied by one or more species.

Ectotympanic: a tiny bone that forms part of the border of the ear drum in mammals; derived from the reptilian *angular*.

Embryo: the developing young animal in the egg or in the womb.

Enamel: the hard crystalline calcium phosphate that forms the outer coating of teeth.

Endemic: local or restricted to a particular area or region.

Endothermic: fully "warm-blooded"; body heat is generated entirely internally, as in mammals and birds.

G

Genus: (*pl.* **Genera**): group of animals having common structural characteristics, distinct from those of all other groups. A genus may contain several species.

Glacial: pertaining to glaciers or glaciated episodes in the history of the Earth.

Grazing: feeding on grasses.

H

Herbivore: plant-eater.

Homologous: a structure present in two or more organisms that arose from the same source.

I

Incisors: the front teeth, generally used for nipping off food.

Incus: the anvil; the middle of the three auditory ossicles in mammals; derived from the reptilian *quadrate*.

Insectivore: insect-eater.

Interglacial: the warm spell between *glacials*.

L

Lagerstätte (*pl.* **Lagerstatten**): site of exceptionally good fossil preservation; for mammals, this includes hair, stomach contents, and even internal organs.

M

Macroevolution: large-scale evolution, occurring mainly over geological time scales.

Malleus: the hammer; the outer of the three auditory ossicles in mammals; derived from the reptilian *articular*.

Marsupials: the pouched mammals, found today mainly in Australia and South America.

Mass extinction: the death of many diverse species worldwide in a relatively short time.

Missing link: a fossil form that apparently fits midway between two major groups.

Molars: the cheek teeth at the back which are used for grinding or shredding food.

Monotremes: the Australasian mammals that still lay eggs.

N

Niche: the role of a species in the environment.

Nocturnal: active at night.

O

Occlusion: position of teeth when jaws are brought together.

Omnivore: an animal that feeds on both plants and flesh.

P

Pelycosaurs: the sail-backed reptiles of the Late Carboniferous and Early Permian that preceded the *therapsids*.

Phylogeny: the pattern of evolution of an animal or plant type.

Placentals: the mammals that retain their young in the womb; the majority of living mammals.

Premolars: the front cheek teeth, just behind the *canines*; premolars are not present in the milk dentition, only the adult.

Q

Quadrate: the bone at the outer lower corner of the reptilian skull which makes contact with the lower jaw; transformed into the *incus* in mammals.

R

Ruminants: mammals that ruminate, or regurgitate and ferment, their food, such as cattle, deer, camels.

S

Squamosal: the bone near the back of the skull which forms the upper angle in reptiles, and forms the jaw joint in mammals.

Stapes: the stirrup; the sole auditory ossicle of reptiles, and the innermost of three in mammals.

Synapsids: the mammal-like reptiles.

T

Temporal opening: the opening(s) behind the eye socket in various amniote skulls.

Therapsids: the later mammal-like reptiles; equals *Synapsids* minus *Pelycosaurs*.

Tundra: frozen glacial soil.

U

Ungulates: hoofed *herbivores*, such as cattle, horses, deer, elephants.

V

Vertebrae: the bony elements of the backbone.

Vertebrates: the animals with backbones, namely fishes, amphibians, reptiles, birds and mammals.

Z

Zygomatic arch: the "cheek bone" of mammals; the bony arch beneath the eye socket and the *temporal opening*.

UNDERSTANDING FOSSIL NAMES

Fossil animals such as mammals and their ancestral group, the mammal-like reptiles, are given scientific names when they are first announced to the world. These names are based on Greek or Latin, and while their meanings are sometimes self-explanatory, often they are harder to guess: generally, however, the name tells us something significant about the animal in question.

Below is a guide to the names of the animals mentioned in this book, giving details of the pronunciation and meaning of each one. The scientists who named each beast, and the date of naming, are also given.

Aegyptopithecus
ee-JIP-toe-PITH-e-kus
Egyptian monkey
E. L. Simons 1965

Aerosaurus
AIR-oh-SAW-rus
Air reptile
A. S. Romer 1937

Afrochoerus
AFF-roe-CHEER-us
African pig
L. S. B. Leakey 1942

Agriochoerus
AG-ree-oh-CHEER-us
Wild pig
J. Leidy 1850

Allodesmus
AL-oh-DEZ-mus
Other chain
R. Kellogg 1922

Alphadon
AL-fa-don
First tooth
G. G. Simpson 1927

Alticamelus
AL-ti-KAM-eh-lus
Tall camel
W. D. Matthew 1924

Amynodon
am-EYE-no-don
Defence tooth
O. C. Marsh 1877

Archaeotherium
AR-kay-oh-THEE-ree-um
Ancient beast
J. Leidy 1850

Archaeothyris
AR-kay-oh-THY-riss
Ancient window
R. R. Reisz 1972

Arctocyon
ARK-toe-KY-on
Bear tooth
H. D. de Blainville 1841

Arsinoitherium
AR-sin-oy-THEE-ree-um
Arsinoë's beast
H. J. L. Beadnell 1920

Astrapotherium
as-TRAP-oh-THEE-ree-um
Lightning beast
H. Burmeister 1879

Australopithecus
o-STRAL-oh-PITH-eh-kus
Southern ape
R. Dart 1925

Basilosaurus
BA-zil-oh-SAW-rus
Royal reptile
R. Harlan 1834

Borhyaena
BOR-hy-EE-na
Northern hyaena
F. Ameghino 1887

Brontotherium
BRON-toe-THEE-ree-um
Thunder beast
W. B. Scott & H. F. Osborn 1887

Buxolestes
BUX-oh-LESS-teez
Plump tooth
J.-J. Jaeger 1970

Chalicotherium
CHAL-i-koe-THEE-ree-um
Pebble beast
J. J. Kaup 1833

Coelodonta
SEEL-oh-DON-ta
Hollow tooth
H. G. Bronn 1831

Cosoryx
KOZE-or-ix
Sharp gazelle
E. D. Cope 1884

Cotylorhynchus
koe-TILE-o-RINK-us
Cup snout
J. W. Stovall 1937

Crusafontia
KROO-sa-FONT-ee-a
Named after Sgr. Crusafont
B. Krebs 1988

Cynognathus
sy-nog-NAY-thus
Dog jaw
H. G. Seeley 1896

Deinogalerix
DINE-oh-GAL-er-ix
Terrible hedgehog
M. Freudenthal 1973

Deinotherium
DINE-oh-THEE-ree-um
Terrible beast
J. J. Kaup 1829

Deltatheridium
DEL-ta-THER-id-ee-um
Little delta beast
W. K. Gregory & G. G. Simpson 1928

Diademodon
DY-a-DEM-oh-don
Crown tooth
H. G. Seeley 1895

Diadiaphorus
DY-a-dy-a-FOR-us
Thoroughly fearless
F. Ameghino 1887

Dimetrodon
dy-MEET-ro-don
Two long teeth
E. D. Cope 1878

Dinictis
DY-nik-tiss
Terrible weasel
J. Leidy 1856

Diprotodon
dy-PROTE-oh-don
Two first teeth
R. Owen 1870

Ectoconus
EK-toe-KONE-us
Internal cone
E. D. Cope 1884

Edaphosaurus
eh-DAF-oh-SAW-rus
Earth reptile
E. D. Cope 1883

Elasmotherium
eh-LAZ-moe-THEE-ree-um
Plate beast
G. Fischer von Waldheim 1809

Entelodon
en-TEL-oh-DON
Perfect teeth
A. Gaudry 1877

Eomanis
EE-oh-MAN-iss
Early pangolin
G. Storch 1978

Epigaulus
ep-i-GAUL-uss
Upon bucket
C. W. Hibbard & L. F. Phillips 1945

Erythrotherium
er-ITH-roe-THEE-ree-um
Red beast
A. W. Crompton 1964

Eurotamandua
YOO-roe-TAM-an-dyoo-a
European ant-eater
G. Storch 1978

Glyptodon
GLIP-toe-don
Carved tooth
R. Owen 1839

Glyptotherium
GLIP-toe-THEE-ree-um
Carved beast
H. F. Osborn 1903

Gomphotherium
GOM-foe-THEE-ree-um
Nail beast
F. Cuvier 1806

Heterohyus
HET-er-oh-HY-us
Different hog
P. Gervais 1848

Hipparion
hip-A-ree-on
Horse
J. Christol 1832

Homo
HOE-moe
Man
C. Linnaeus 1758

Hyaenodon
hy-EE-no-don
Hyaena tooth
M. de Laizer & L. de Parieu 1838

Hyopsodus
HY-op-SODE-us
Hog tooth
J. Leidy 1870

Hypertragulus
HY-per-TRAG-yoo-luss
Upper small goat
E. D. Cope 1873

Hyracotherium
HY-rak-oh-THEE-ree-um
Hyrax beast
R. Owen 1841

Icaronycteris
IK-ar-oh-NIK-ter-iss
Icarus bat
L. E. Russell & D. E. Savage 1973

Kamptobaatar
KAMP-toe-BA-tar
Bend (mammal from Ulan Bator Mongolia)
Z. Kielan-Jaworowska 1970

Leptictidium
lep-TIK-tid-EE-um
Thin weasel
H. Tobien 1962

Leptictis
lep-TIK-tis
Thin weasel
J. Leidy 1868

Lophiodon
LOAF-ee-oh-DON
Crest tooth
G. Cuvier 1822

Lystrosaurus
LIST-roe-SAW-rus
Spoon reptile
E. D. Cope 1870

Machairodus
MAK-ire-ODE-us
Sword tooth
J. Kaup 1833

Macrauchenia
MAK-row-CHEEN-ee-a
Large neck
R. Owen 1856

Mammuthus
MAM-uh-thus
Burrower
J. F. Burmeister 1803

Megaloceros
MEG-al-O-ser-os
Great horn
J. F. Blumenbach 1803

Megathcrium
MEG-a-THEE-ree-um
Big beast
R. Owen 1856

Megazostrodon
MEG-a-ZOS-troe-don
Big girdle tooth
A. W. Crompton & F. R.
Jenkins 1968

Megistotherium
MEG-iss-tro-THEE-ree-um
Very big beast
R. Savage 1973

Mcrychippus
MER-ee-KIP-us
Ruminant horse
J. Leidy 1856

Merycoidodon
MER-ee-KOID-oh-don
Ruminant form tooth
J. Leidy 1848

Mesohippus
MEEZ-oh-HIP-us
Middle horse
O. C. Marsh 1875

Mesonyx
MEEZ-on-ix
Middle claw
E. D. Cope 1878

Messelobunodon
MESS-ell-oh-BYOON-oh-don
Messel rounded-hill tooth
H. Franzen 1980

Moeritherium
MER-i-THEE-ree-um
Part beast
C. W. Andrews 1906

Morganucodon
MOR-gan-YOOK-oh-don
Morgan's tooth
W. G. Kühne 1949

Moschops
MOS-kops
Calf eye
R. Broom 1911

Necrolemur
NEK-roe-LEEM-ur
Dead lemur
H. Filhol 1883

Neohipparion
NEE-oh-HIP-ar-ee-on
New *Hipparion*
J. W. Gidley 1903

Nimravus
NIM-rav-uss
Excessive grey-yellow
E. D. Cope 1879

Obdurodon
ob-DYOO-roe-don
Hardened tooth
M. O. Woodburne & R. H.
Tedford 1975

Ophiacodon
OAF-ee-AK-oh-don
Snake tooth
O. C. Marsh 1878

Oudenodon
oo-DEN-oh-don
Nothing tooth
R. Owen 1860

Oxyaena
OX-eye-EE-na
Sharp hyaena
E. D. Cope 1874

Pakicetus
PAK-i-SEET-us
Pakistan whale
P. D. Gingerich & D. E.
Russell 1981

Palaeocastor
PALE-ee-oh-KAS-tor
Ancient beaver
J. Leidy 1856

Palaeochiropteryx
PALE-ee-oh-KIRE-op-ter-ix
Ancient bat
H. Revilliod 1917

Palaeolagus
PALE-ee-LAG-uss
Ancient rabbit
J. Leidy 1856

Palorchestes
PALL-or-CHESS-teez
Wandering beast
R. Owen 1873

Phenacodus
fen-AK-oh-dus
Impostor tooth
E. D. Cope 1873

Platybelodon
PLAT-ee-BEL-oh-don
Flat dart
tooth
A. A. Borissiak 1928

Plesiadapis
PLEEZ-ee-a-DAP-is
Near *Adapis*
P. Gervais 1877

Pliohippus
PLY-oh-HIP-us
Pliocene horse
J. Leidy 1869

Poebrotherium
PEE-bro-THEE-ree-um
Grass-eating horse
J. Leidy 1847

Potamotherium
POT-am-oh-THEE-ree-um
River beast
E. Geoffroy St-Hilaire
1833

Probelesodon
pro-BEL-eez-o-don
Before fine-tooth
A. S. Romer 1962

Proconsul
pro-KON-sul
Before Consul

Procynosuchus
pro-KINE-oh-SOOK-us
Before dog-reptile
R. Broom 1937

Propalaeotherium
pro-PAIL-ee-oh-THEE-ree-um
Before ancient-beast
H. de Blainville 1846

Prothylacynus
pro-THY-lak-INE-uss
Before pouched
F. Ameghino 1891

Ptilodus
till-ODE-uss
Feather tooth
E. D. Cope 1881

Rakomeryx
rak-OM-er-ix
Ragged ruminant
C. Frick 1937

Ramapithecus
ram-a-PITH-e-kus
Rama ape
G. E. Pilgrim 1910

Ramoceros
RAM-o-SER-os
Branched horn
W. D. Matthew 1904

Roberthoffstetteria
ROB-ert-HOFF-stet-EE-ree-a
Robert Hoffstetter
L. G. Marshal & C. de Muizon
1988

Samotherium
SAME-oh-THEE-ree-um
Samos beast
C. I. Forsyth-Major 1888

Sinclairella
SIN-klair-ELL-a
W. B. Sinclair
G. Jepsen 1934

Sinclairomeryx
SIN-klair-O-mer-ix
Sinclair's ungulate
W. B. Sinclair & C. Frick
1937

Sinopa
SINE-ope-a
REd earth
J. Leidy 1872

Sivapithecus
SEEV-a-PITH-e-kus
Siva ape
G. E. Pilgrim 1915

Sivatherium
SEEV-a-THEE-ree-um
Siva beast
H. Falconer & P. Cautley
1836

Smilodon
SMILE-oh-don
Chisel tooth
J. Leidy 1868

Squalodon
SKWAL-oh-don
Whale tooth
J. P. S. Grateloup 1840

Stegodon
STEG-oh-don
Spine tooth
H. Falconer 1857

Stylinodon
STY-lin-OH-don
Pillar tooth
O. C. Marsh 1874

Synthetoceras
SIN-thet-O-ser-as
Compound skull
R. A. Stirton 1932

Thrinaxodon
thrin-AX-oh-don
Trident tooth
H. G. Seeley 1894

Thylacinus
THY-lak-INE-us
Pouched
G. Harris 1808

Thylacoleo
THY-lak-oh-LEE-oh
Pouched lion
R. Owen 1859

Thylacosmilus
THY-lak-oh-SMILE-uss
Pouched chisel
E. S. Riggs 1933

Titanoides
TITE-an-OID-eez
Titanic
C. W. Gidley 1917

Trigonias
TRIG-own-EE-ass
Three-angled
F. A. Lucas 1900

Uintatherium
YOO-in-ta-THEE-ree-um
Uinta beast
J. Leidy 1872

Zalambdalestes
zal-AM-da-LESS-teez
Very lambda-toothed
Z. Kielan-Jaworowska
1978

Zygomaturus
ZIGE-oh-MA-too-russ
Cheek bone arch
W. S. Macleay 1857

Zygorhiza
ZIGE-oh-RIZE-a
Twin root
H. G. Seeley 1878

INDEX

CREDITS

Quarto would like to thank the following for their help with this publication and for permission to reproduce copyright material.

p7 Mary Evans Picture Library; **p8** Mary Evans Picture Library; **p9** Mansell Collection; **p10** Mansell Collection; **p11** Mary Evans Picture Library; **p12** Mansell Collection; **p13** (*top right*) Mansell Collection, (*bottom left*) Mary Evans Picture Library; **p17** South Africa Museum/ Dr G M King; **p18** Erindale College/ Dr R R Reisz; **p19** Erindale College/ Dr R R Reisz; **p22** (*top left*) Dr Donald Baird, (*bottom left*) South Africa Museum/ Dr G M King; **p23** South Africa Museum/ Dr G M King; **p26** Witwatersrand/ Dr C E Gow; **p27** (*top*) Dr Donald Baird, (*below*) Witwatersrand/ Dr C E Gow; **p29** (*top*) South Africa Museum/ Dr G M King, (*below*) Geology Dept. Univ. Bristol/Professor R J G Savage; **p31** Dr Donald Baird; **p32** (*top*) Professor R J G Savage, (*below*) Geology Dept. Univ. Bristol/Professor R J G Savage; **p37** Freie Universität Berlin/Bernard Krebs; **p38** Dr D W Krause; **p39** W Skarzynski; **p41** Forschungsinstitut/ Dr G Storch; **p42** Dr D W Krause; **p43** Institut für Palaontologie der Universität, Bonn/ Dr Wighart V Koenigswald; **p44** Dr Donald Baird; **p48** The John Hopkins University/ Dr K D Rose; **p50** Dr Donald Baird; **p51** Geology Dept. Univ. Bristol/Professor R J G Savage; **p52** Dr Donald Baird; **p54** Dr Donald Baird; **p55** Forschungsinstitut Senckenberg/Haupt; **p58** (*left*) P Morris, (*right*) Forschungsinstitut Senckenberg/ Haupt; **p59** Forschungsinstitut Senckenberg/Haupt; **p60** Forschungsinstitut Senckenberg/Haupt; **p61** Forschungsinstitut/ Dr G Storch; **p63** Natural History Museum of Los Angeles/Marcus Schneck; **p67** Dr Donald Baird; **p70** (*left*) Dr Donald Baird, (*right*) P Morris; **p75** Dr Donald Baird; **p76** (*top left*) Dr Donald Baird, (*below right*) Brown University/Christine Janis; **p78** Brown University/Christine Janis; **p79** (*bottom left*) Dr Donald Baird; **p80** Dr Donald Baird; **p81** University of Otago/ R Ewan Fordyce; **p85** P Morris; **p88** Neville Pledge; **p89** Neville Pledge; **p90** (*top*) Museum of Victoria/Thomas Rich, (*below*) Neville Pledge; **p91** Australia House; **p92** (*top right*) Dr Donald Baird; **p97** State of Utah/ Cicllette; **p98** (*top*) State of Utah/ Cicllette; **p99** (*top left*) Professor R J G Savage; **p100** P Morris; **p101** Professor R J G Savage; **p103** Dr Donald Baird; **p104** (*left*) Brown University/Christine Janis, (*right*) Geology Dept. Univ. Bristol/ Professor R J G Savage; **p105** Geology Dept. Univ. Bristol/ Professor R J G Savage; **p106** (*left*) Brown University/Christine Janis, (*right*) Geology Dept. Univ. Bristol/Professor R J G Savage; **p109** (*top*) Brown University/Christine Janis, (*below right*) P Morris; **p110** Brown University/Christine Janis; **p111** Brown University/Christine Janis; **p112** (*top right*) Brown University/Christine Janis; **p113** (*top right*) Professor R J G Savage; **p114** (*top left*) Elephant Interest Group/ Jeheskel Shoshani; **p119** Elephant Interest Group/ Jeheskel Shoshani; **p120** P Morris; **p121** Elephant Interest Group/ Jeheskel Shoshani; **p123** Institute of Human Origins; **p125** G S F Picture Library; **p126** (*top*) G S F Picture Library, (*below*) Elephant Interest Group/ Jeheskel Shoshani; **p127** Secol, Thetford; **p132** (*top*) Smithsonian Institute, (*bottom left*) Dr Donald Baird, (*below right*) Nick Buzzard; **p133** Smithsonian Museum; **p134** Professor R J G Savage; **p135** Elephant Interest Group/ Jeheskel Shoshani; **p137** Visual Arts Library.

Dinosaur Reconstructions: Graham Rosewarne; skeletal diagrams: Jim Robins; charts and diagrams: Janos Marffy, David Kemp and Sally Launder.

Every effort has been made to trace and acknowledge all copyright holders. Quarto would like to apologize if any omissions have been made.